For the Love of Lucy

Love Always
Lucille

For the Love of Lucy

The Complete Guide for Collectors and Fans

Ric B. Wyman

Abbeville Press ♥ Publishers
New York ♥ London ♥ Paris

To Linda Peterson,
who helped me say good-bye.
And especially to my parents, Gary and Bernie Wyman,
who've shown me the value of confidence and determination.

♥   ♥   ♥

FRONT COVER: From the cover of *TV Guide*, January 25–31, 1952 (see page 16).
BACK COVER: Black-and-white photograph: Lucille Ball, 1940s; counterclockwise from top right: *V*, October 12, 1947, France (see also page 140); *TV Guide*, March 1–7, 1969 (see also page 22); press book for MGM's *Ziegfeld Follies of 1946* (see also page 74); *Look*, April 21, 1953 (see also page 122); "I Love Lucy" Lucy Ricardo rag doll, 1953 (see also page 57); Dixie-cup lid, 1943 (see also page 100).

EDITOR: Jacqueline Decter
DESIGNER: Celia Fuller
PRODUCTION EDITOR: Owen Dugan
PRODUCTION MANAGER: Lou Bilka
PHOTO STYLIST: Frederick J. Latasa
Memorabilia photographs by Image Studios

First edition
10 9 8 7 6 5 4 3 2 1

Use of "I Love Lucy" photographs on pages 104, 136, and 154 courtesy of CBS Inc.

All of the items reproduced in this book are from private collections. Grateful acknowledgment is made to the original producers of the photographed materials. Whenever possible, the copyright for each item has been identified. If any omission or incorrect information is found, it should be given to the author or publisher and it will be amended in any future edition of the book.

As the values for items pictured in this book are approximations, neither the author nor the publisher shall be held responsible for any losses that may occur through the consultation of this book in the purchase or sale of items.

LIBRARY OF CONGRESS CATALOGING-IN-PUBLICATION DATA
Wyman, Ric B.
   For the love of Lucy : the complete guide for collectors and fans / Ric B. Wyman.
       p.   cm.
   Includes bibliographical references and index.
   ISBN 0-7892-0006-6
   1. Ball, Lucille, 1911–   —Collectibles. I. Title.
PN2287.B16W96   1995
791'.45'028'092—dc20   94-49002

Acknowledgments

For the Love of Lucy has certainly been a collaborative effort. My sincere appreciation is extended to those whose support, contributions, and encouragement are reflected indirectly on its pages. They include, but are not limited to: Jane Elliott; Belva and Mike Simonis; Archie and Sue Hansen; Robby Wyman (who proved me wrong in a K-Mart parking lot); Bekki Wyman; Kieth Dodge and Elisabeth Edwards at Arluck Entertainment; Tom Watson; Marty Garcia at CBS; Jim Moloshok, Greg Berutto, and Jyll Gartin at Warner Brothers; Linda Peterson; David Geboy; Jerry and Sharon Geboy; Lucille Heath; Marge "The Peddler" Dobeck (for getting me started); my friends at Prange Way in Wausau; Norman and Marion Van Vlack; Sam and Doris Paladino; the people of the Lucille Ball Little Theatre of Jamestown; Bart Andrews; Rick Carl; Harold Stepper; Patty Speen; Debbie Schott; Eric Olson; Mary Tsosie; Lois HuiZar; Val DeCarlo; Don Aston; Dave Siegel; Brad Miller and the Thousand Oaks Library; Gregg Oppenheimer (for his insights into and generous contributions to the "My Favorite Husband" log); Philip and Lenore Levine; and my old college roommate, Keith Janke, who humbly dealt with my TV viewing habits while this book was in the early stages of development.

To the countless Lucy fans who've been patiently awaiting the arrival of this book, thank you for your enthusiasm.

Special thanks to the following individuals who provided insights and advised me: Pat Klug, Cathy Ladd, Patrick McGilligan, and Larry Watson; and to those whose contributions made an impact on what you see: Fred Latasa and Image Studio's Dave Wallace, Krystal Behrens, and Dave Aschenbrenner.

In order to make this book as complete as possible, I asked several people to lend items from their personal collections for photography purposes. My thanks to the following for their generosity and trust: Michael Stern (Lucy's no. 1 fan), Patti Pesavento, Pam Gragg, Richard Tususian, Sue Buetow, and Cari Purkey. And to Ted Hake of Hake's Americana and Tambre Clarke of Hamilton Gifts, thank you both for the special effort. (The specific items these people lent are listed on page 224.)

My appreciation is also sent to the people at Abbeville Press who recognized the potential of this project. Special thanks to Celia Fuller for her outstanding design; to Nadine Winns, "The Voice of Abbeville," who was always there to take my calls; and especially to my editor, Jackie Decter, who listened to my concerns, provided invaluable positive feedback, and influenced the final product in such a significant way.

My unending gratitude to Lucie Arnaz, who believed in my work and helped make it all happen. Thanks, Lucie.

To those I may have inadvertently slighted by omission, my deepest apologies.

And finally, to my parents, Gary and Bernie Wyman, my love and thanks for supporting my ideas and encouraging me in all my ventures.

Ric Wyman
January 1995

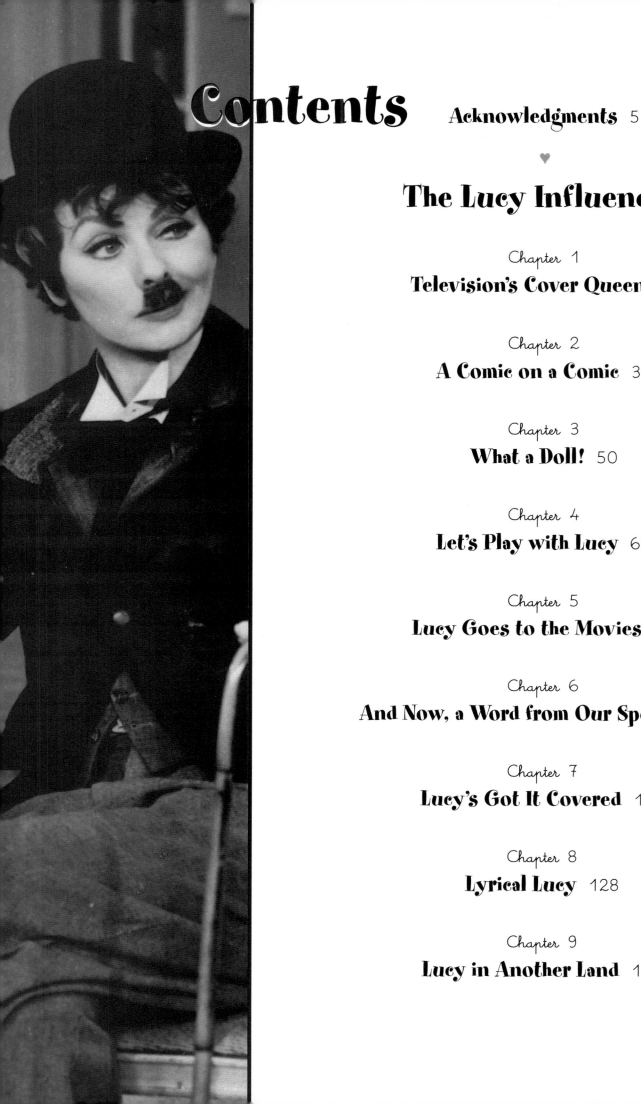

Contents

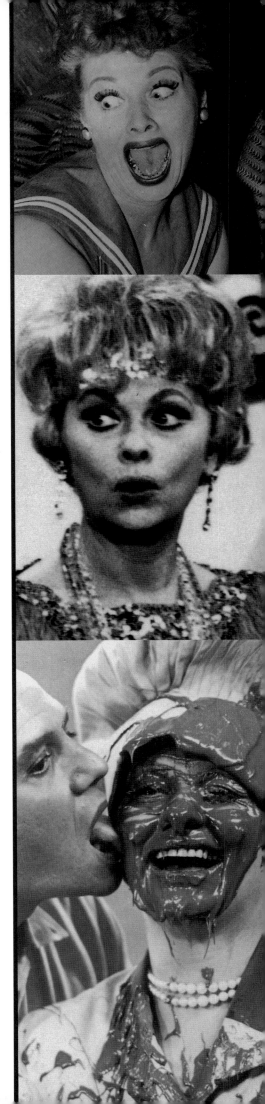

The Lucy Influence

She was wrapping chocolates when I first saw her. With her friend Ethel by her side, she worked frantically, becoming ever more frazzled as the candy began whizzing by her on the assembly line. But she wouldn't be defeated. Determined to keep her job, she stuffed the unfinished work down her blouse, in her hat, and in her mouth before her boss walked in.

I was too young to know that the program I had just watched had become an enduring television classic. I was still laughing as the big heart appeared and the credits rolled up the screen, so I knew I'd be back for another visit with the hilarious lady living in the land of black and white. The more I saw her, the more she fascinated me. Over time, my childhood delight developed into a deep appreciation for the comic genius of Lucille Ball.

Some years ago, I visited a little antiques shop in Wausau, a city not far from my hometown. While browsing through artifacts of America past, I came across a children's storybook, *Lucy and the Madcap Mystery*, sandwiched between a pair of old bookends. Pictured on the cover was that same redhead with whom I had spent so many afternoons as a child. The book was old, the pages discolored, and a name was written in a child's hand inside the front cover—all elements that made it even more interesting. Not realizing that I was about to embark upon a decade-long adventure, I decided to buy it. As I walked away from that little secondhand store, I began to wonder what other items related to Lucy might be out there waiting to be rediscovered. And so it started.

With some kind of archaeological instinct, I set off to unearth Lucy artifacts. Each piece I found told me something new about the legendary lady. Magazine covers from the 1930s to the 1990s illustrated her extraordinary popularity. Paint brochures, toothpaste cartons, and countless magazine and newspaper advertisements for the many products she endorsed indicated that she had earned the public's trust. Coloring books, comic books, paper dolls, and board games attested to her appeal among children, while the covers of French, Italian, Mexican, British, and other foreign movie magazines proved that she was a star of international renown. Each item captures a little bit of the ineffable quality that made her America's most beloved funny lady; collectively they reveal her enormous impact and influence on American popular culture. As *TV Guide* once claimed, the face of Lucille Ball has been "seen by more people more often than the face of any human being who ever lived."

She was goofy but charming. She was gorgeous yet madcap. With a mere blink of her huge blue eyes or twist of her lips, her remarkable face could express everything from agony to zaniness. She schemed and connived with uncanny ingenuity to get what she wanted, and then wailed endearingly when her plans inevitably backfired. The more outlandish her predicaments, the more she made us laugh. And the more we laughed, the more we loved her. We laughed for the love of Lucy.

Lucille Ball, 1960s

Lucille Ball Memorabilia
Value Guide

Each piece of memorabilia featured in *For the Love of Lucy* has been assigned a letter indicating its approximate value. The letters represent the following price ranges:

A = $0–25   E = $350–700
B = $25–75   F = $700–1,200
C = $75–150   G = $1,200+
D = $150–350

To determine value, the following factors were taken into consideration: current market demand, availability, rarity, past actual winning auction bids, varying dealer prices, and the author's personal experience. The values assigned are for information purposes only.

♥   ♥   ♥

Condition

The condition of an item greatly influences its worth. Because vintage Hollywood items were originally not intended to become nostalgic keepsakes, they are usually found in worn condition. Old movie magazines were often cut up with scissors, movie posters were manhandled by theater administrators, and TV-show coloring books were colored in. Paper dolls were cut and torn, comic books were rolled up and carried in back pockets, and over the years board games lost their pieces. Heavy wear, defacement, or soiling all reduce the value of such items considerably.

Television's Cover Queen

In the summer of 1991 the nation's top-selling weekly magazine, *TV Guide*, published a special-edition two-thousandth issue honoring the greatest stars of television's history. And who more appropriate to be featured on the cover of this oversize issue than the redhead who has graced *TV Guide*'s cover more often than anyone else—a lady named Lucy. Two years later, in the December 18–24, 1993, issue, the magazine celebrated its fortieth year in national circulation, and Lucy was pictured on the cover once again to help commemorate this milestone of Americana.

With an impressive thirty-six covers to her credit, Lucille Ball reigns as *TV Guide*'s cover queen. Sometimes she appears alone. Other times she's seen with her husband and costar Desi Arnaz. She even shared the cover with a dolphin named Splash on one occasion in 1965. But no matter who she's pictured with or what she's doing, one thing comes through all the covers—the lady has the magic to make people laugh.

As early as 1948 primitive forms of *TV Guide* and similar weekly TV-listing magazines could be found in select regions of the United States. *TV Digest, Television Week, TV Forecast,* and *TV Dial* are just a few of the many other regional television program guides in circulation during television's infancy. Today they are quite scarce and can command high prices from nostalgia collectors. Lucille Ball was featured on the covers of several of these fledgling TV-listing magazines throughout the early 1950s, including at least five appearances on cover of the prenational *TV Guide*.

Her first appearance on *TV Guide*'s cover occurred during the same week "I Love Lucy" made its television debut—the week of October 12, 1951. Lucy is in good company here, sharing the cover spot with Bob Hope, Danny Thomas, Abbott and Costello, and husband Desi Arnaz. At the time no one had any idea what a lasting impression she was about to make.

The following year Lucy could be found on the cover of four more prenational *TV Guide* issues. On January 25 and June 6, 1952, she and Desi were featured together. On September 12 Lucy and Milton Berle occupied the cover space. And at year's end, on December 19, Lucy shared the cover with Howdy Doody, Jackie Gleason, Roy Rogers, Ed Sullivan, and several other big names of the time.

On April 3, 1953, *TV Guide* published its first nationally distributed issue, its first step on the way to becoming the single most prominent source for television program information. This first nationwide issue features Lucille Ball and her "$50,000,000 baby," Desi Arnaz Jr., and is considered to be the most valuable of all *TV Guides*—worth as much as $2,000 in perfect condition.

Later that same year *TV Guide* did a cover story on Lucy and Desi's current motion picture project, *The Long, Long Trailer,* providing a sneak peek at the film. Future issues caught Lucy jumping over a potted plant, swimming with a dolphin, going "mod in London," and posing with her children, Lucie and Desi Jr.

In 1970 *TV Guide* was the first periodical to give America a glimpse of a now-classic "Here's Lucy" episode featuring Elizabeth Taylor and Richard Burton. The September 5, 1970, issue, featuring a candid cover shot of Lucy and the Burtons, served as a preview to the third season of "Here's Lucy."

Throughout Lucy's reign as television's comedy queen, other TV-listing magazines also featured her likeness on their covers. Found sandwiched between the sections of the Sunday newspaper, these program guides became an added bonus for newspaper subscribers. Compared to *TV Guide*, these supplements were often larger in size but usually contained fewer pages and lacked the entertainment news and insights *TV Guide* has become renowned for.

Like most collectibles, the value of vintage TV-listing magazines is in part determined by their age and condition. Consumer demand also influences their market value. In recent years *TV Guide* has become an increasingly popular collectible. More and more often people search for particular issues to give as gifts commemorating a birthday, anniversary, or other special day in a friend or family member's life. Old *TV Guides* not only represent the pop culture of the time but also help document exactly what we were watching the morning Robby was born or the day Karen and Kenny got married.

Because of this resurgence of interest in expired *TV Guides*, collectors of Lucille Ball nostalgia often find themselves competing with others when trying to locate specific issues—and sometimes pay a high price to add that special issue to their collections. So the next time you begin to go through the weekly ritual of tossing away that old *TV Guide*, take a minute and consider the potential of what you're carrying to the trash.

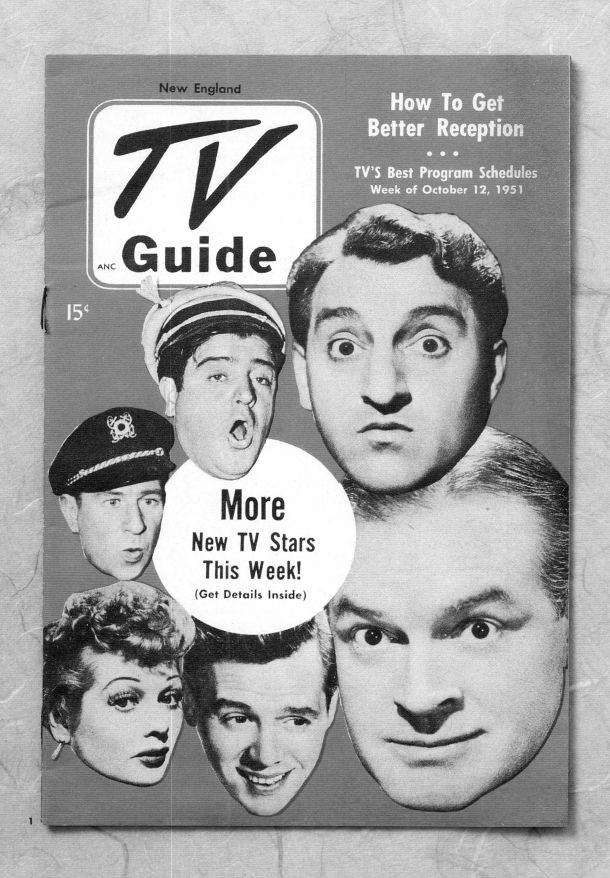

1. *TV Guide*, October 12–18, 1951 (D)

DEC. 19-25 PROGRAMS — See the Great Christmas Shows

TV Guide

15¢

SPECIAL ISSUE!
Our Annual Awards

TV GUIDE
GOLD MEDAL
AWARD

Who are
the BEST in television?

2

2. *TV Guide*, December 19–25, 1952 (D)

3. *TV Guide,*
January 25–31, 1952 (D)

4. *TV Guide,*
June 6–12, 1952 (D)

5. *TV Guide,*
September 12–18, 1952 (D)

LUCY AND DESI TACKLE THE MOVIES

TV GUIDE

The Truth About Television Snobs

COMPLETE PROGRAM LISTINGS
Week of July 17-23

15¢

GOD BLESS OUR HOME

6

6. *TV Guide,*
July 17–23, 1953 (C/D)

TV RATINGS—FACT OR FRAUD?

TV GUIDE

COMPLETE PROGRAM LISTINGS
Week of April 17-23

15¢

7

7. *TV Guide,*
April 17–23, 1953 (C/D)

HOW TV CHANGED LUCILLE BALL

TV GUIDE

LOCAL PROGRAM LISTINGS
Week of April 23—29

15¢

Lucille Ball

8

8. *TV Guide,*
April 23–29, 1954 (C)

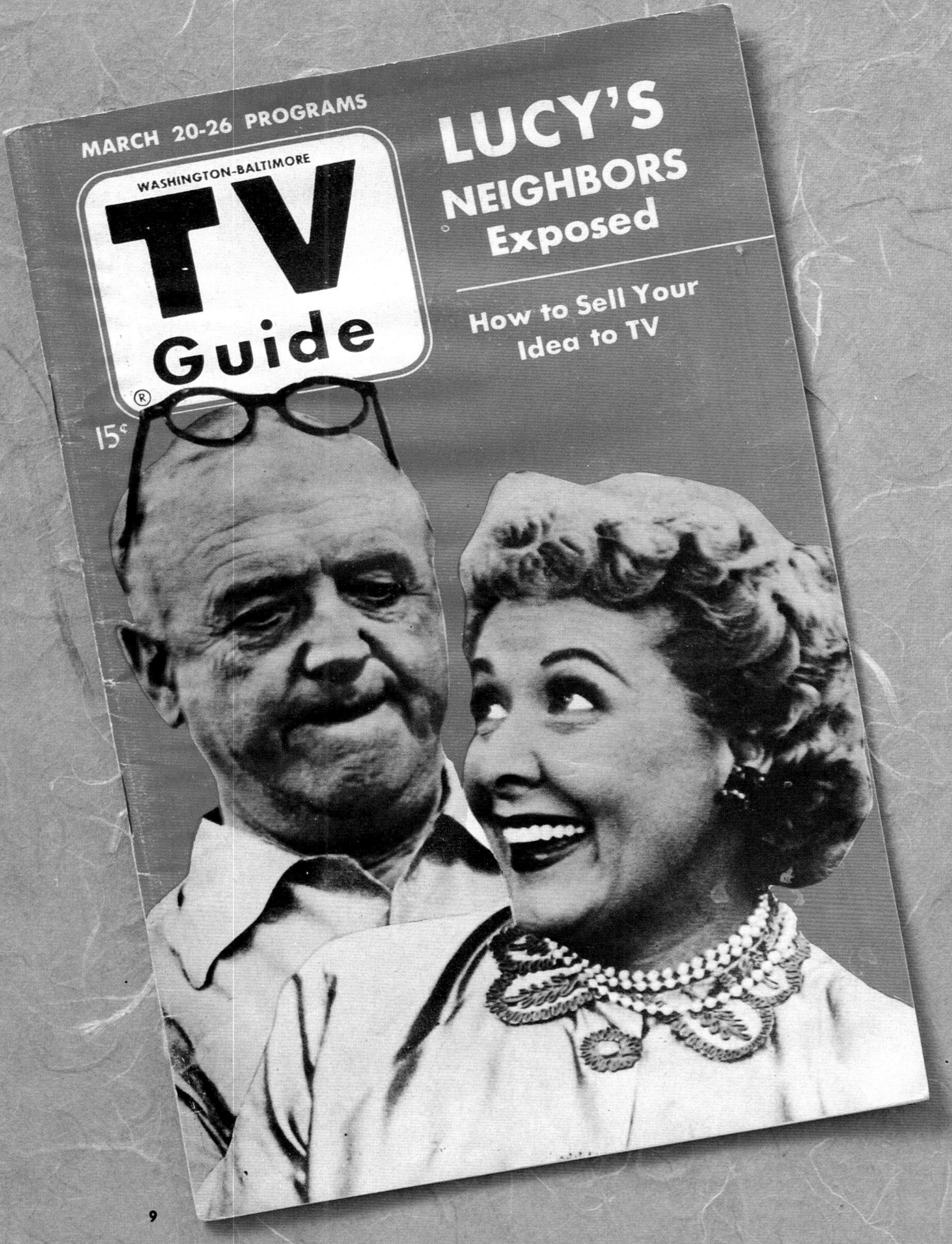

MARCH 20-26 PROGRAMS
WASHINGTON-BALTIMORE
TV Guide
15¢
LUCY'S
NEIGHBORS
Exposed
How to Sell Your
Idea to TV

9

9. *TV Guide*, March 20–26, 1953 (D)

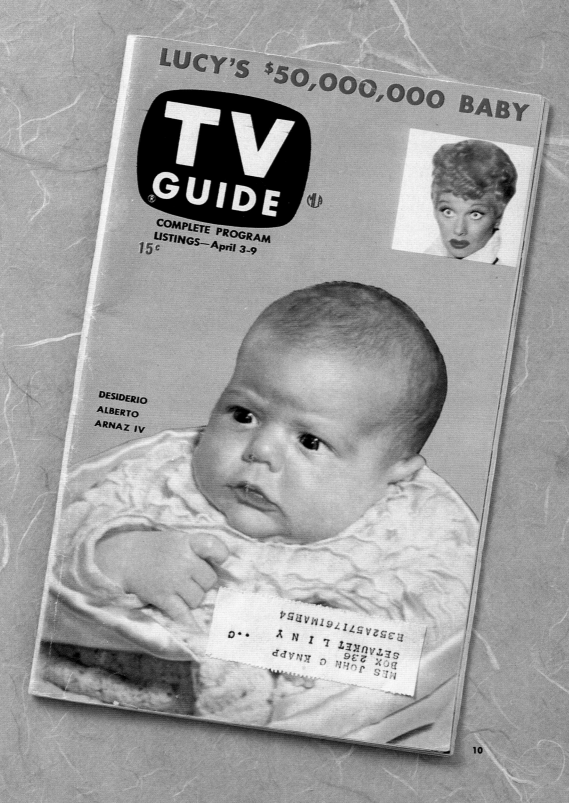

10. *TV Guide*, April 3–9, 1953; the first national issue (F/G)

11. *TV Guide,* July 12–18, 1958 (C)
12. *TV Guide,*
December 10–16, 1955 (C)
13. *TV Guide,* October 9–15, 1954 (C)

14. *TV Guide,*
January 12–18, 1957 (C)
15. *TV Guide,* November 2–8, 1957 (C)
16. *TV Guide,* July 30–August 5, 1955 (B/C)

20 ♥ **Television's Cover Queen**

17. *TV Guide*,
April 30–May 6, 1966 (B)
18. *TV Guide*, July 16–22, 1960 (B/C)
19. *TV Guide*, April 6–12, 1963 (B)

SUMMER TV: THEY'RE TRYING SOME <u>NEW</u> SHOWS!
see page 5

TV GUIDE

LOCAL PROGRAMS
APRIL 30–MAY 6
15¢

Ronald Searle
sketches
Lucille Ball
see page 19

LUCILLE BALL: HUMILIATED AND UNHAPPY
Local Listings · July 16-22

TV GUIDE
15¢

LUCILLE BALL

18

Special—DO YOU REMEMBER?...
On our 10th anniversary
TV Guide calls the roll
of 10 memorable years

TV GUIDE
LOCAL PROGRAMS
APRIL 6–12
15¢

19

TV GUIDE
LOCAL PROGRAMS · SEPT. 29–OCT. 5
15¢

■ LUCY CLOWNS AGAIN
WORLD SERIES DETAILS
■ THE SHOW NOBODY WANTED
■ CASEYITIS Part 2
BROOKS

20

Exclusive:
NEWTON MINOW'S
PROPOSALS FOR
RESHAPING TV
see page 4

TV GUIDE
Local Programs
Sept. 5-11
15¢

The change in
LUCILLE BALL
by Richard Gehman
see page 16

21

TV GUIDE
LOCAL PROGRAMS · AUG. 28–SEPT. 3
15¢

Who's Who
and
What's What
in
'Peyton Place'

AQUATIC STARS:
LUCILLE BALL AND SPLASH

22

20. *TV Guide*,
September 29–October 5, 1962 (B/C)

21. *TV Guide*, September 5–11, 1964 (B)

22. *TV Guide*, August 28–September 3, 1965 (B/C)

23

26

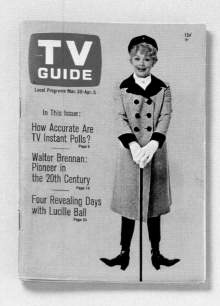

28

23. *TV Guide,*
October 22–28, 1966 (B)

24. *TV Guide,*
March 1–7, 1969 (B)

25. *TV Guide,*
September 5–11, 1970 (B)

24

26. *TV Guide,*
July 15–21, 1967 (B)

27. *TV Guide,*
June 12–18, 1971 (B)

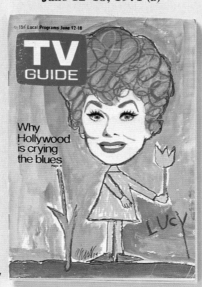

27

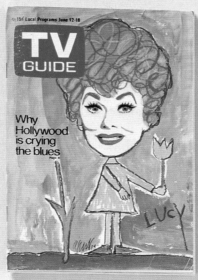

29

25

28. *TV Guide,* March 30–
April 5, 1968 (B)

29. *TV Guide,* March 31–
April 6, 1973 (B)

30. *TV Guide,*
July 6–12, 1974 (B)

30

31. *TV Guide,*
October 4–10,
1986 (A/B)

32. *TV Guide,*
December 16–22,
1989 (A)

33. *TV Guide,*
March 12–18,
1988 (A)

35. *TV Guide,*
May 6–12,
1989 (A)

36. *TV Guide,*
February 9–15,
1991 (A)

37. *TV Guide,*
December 18–24,
1993 (A)

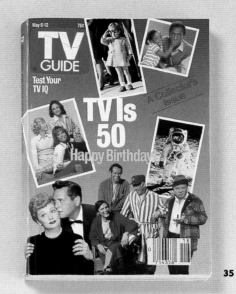

34. *TV Guide* 2,000th
issue, Commemorative
Edition, summer
1991 (A/B)

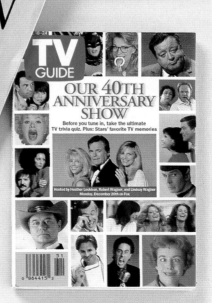

Television's Cover Queen ♥ 23

PROGRAMS · PEOPLE · WEEK OF APRIL 8 - 14

New York Herald Tribune
SECTION 9

TV and Radio Magazine

DESI and LUCY—
THEY'RE BIG
BUSINESS

38

38. *New York Herald Tribune TV and Radio Magazine,*
April 8–14, 1956 (D)

39. *The Chicago Sun Times TV Prevue;*
December 29, 1957–January 4, 1958 (D)

Complete Daily Listings for KSTP-TV & WCCO-TV

1952

NOW 32 PAGES

NOV. 29 THRU DEC. 5

TV FORECAST NORTHWEST AREA

LUCILLE BALL
She Fooled Hollywood

40

43. Before *TV Guide* went national, many regions around the country developed their own TV-listing magazines, such as the Cincinnati-Dayton-Columbus *TV Dial*, October 18–24, 1952 (D)

40. *TV Forecast,* November 29–December 5, 1952 (D)

41. *New York Herald Tribune TV and Radio Magazine,* November 3–9, 1957 (D)

42. *Television Week,* May 31–June 6, 1952 (D)

How TV's Top Show Is Produced • page 16

Cincinnati Dayton Columbus

TV DIAL OCTOBER 18, 1952

complete, advance
TV PROGRAMS

15¢

43

PROGRAMS - PEOPLE - WEEK OF N

NEW YORK
Herald Tribune
SECTION 9

TV and Radio
Magazine

DESI & LUCY
MAKE THE
BIG CHANGE

41

TELEVISION WEEK 10¢

Complete
TV Programs

MAY 31 TO JUNE 6

Lucille Ball
--SEE PAGES 8-9

42

44. *New York Tribune TV and Radio Magazine,* May 22–28, 1955 (C/ D)

• PEOPLE • Week of May 22-28

Tribune TV and Radio
Magazine

AUDREY MEADOWS
LUCILLE BALL
ARLENE FRANCIS
JEAN HAGEN
MARY HEALY
JANIS PAIGE

TV'S FAMOUS
REDHEADS

NANETTE FABRAY

44

WIN WORLD SERIES TICKETS IN FASCINATING BASEBALL CONTEST!

Tops in TV Listings
Week of August 9

VISITING THE TV STARS ON VACATION

EVINRUDE

15¢

45

45. *TV Digest,*
August 9–15, 1952 (C/D)

46. *TV Digest,*
October 20–26, 1951 (D/E)

47. *TV Reporter,*
June 5–11, 1953 (D)

SPECIAL AWARDS ISSUE!
Week of May 24

TV DIGEST 1952

15¢

POPULARITY POLL WINNERS

48

JUNE 5-11 PROGRAMS   HOAGY CARMICHAEL PREMIERE-JUNE 6

TV reporter

GODFREY SAVED MY LIFE - Frank Parker

SPECIAL CHILDREN'S PULL-OUT SECTION

15¢
ANC

WHY LUCY AND DESI ARE
MARRIED FOR KEEPS

HARRIET VAN HORNE REVIEWS NEW TV SHOWS

47

NEW "EYE"
KANE–LL...

TV DIG...

15¢
TV PROGRAMS
WEEK OF
OCTOBER 20th

Lucille Ball of "I Love Lucy"...see page 12

46

...neup—GIMBELS THANKSGIVING DAY PARADE

TV DIGEST

WIN A TRIP TO HOWDY DOODY'S PEANUT GALLERY

Week of November 22

15¢

LUCILLE AND DESI SOLVE A PARENT PROBLEM

49

48. *TV Digest,*
May 24–30, 1952 (D)

49. *TV Digest,*
November 22–28,
1952 (C/D)

50. *Chicago Tribune TV Week,*
April 18–24, 1964 (C)

51. *Chicago Tribune TV Week,*
May 16–22, 1964 (B/C)

52. *Chicago Tribune TV*
Week, October 5–11,
1963 (C)

53. *Chicago Daily Tribune TV Week,*
November 17–23, 1956 (C)

54. *Chicago Daily Tribune TV Week,*
November 2–8, 1957 (C)

55. *Chicago Tribune TV Week,*
March 19–25, 1966 (B/C)

56. *Chicago Tribune TV Week,*
December 30, 1967–
January 5, 1968 (C)

57. *Chicago Tribune TV*
Week, January 16–22,
1965 (C)

58. *Chicago Tribune TV Week,*
June 4–10, 1966 (B/C)

59. *Chicago Tribune TV Week,*
May 2–8, 1970 (C)

July 1 TO July 7 1962

SUNDAY TV NEWS week

LUCILLE BALL & FRIENDS

ENQUIRER TV MAGAZINE

DAILY LISTINGS

ALMOST EVERYONE LOVES LUCY

Week of June 21-27, 1981

60. Sunday News TV Week, July 1–7, 1962 (B)

61. Cincinnati Enquirer TV Magazine, June 21–27, 1981 (B)

61

64. St. Louis Post-Dispatch TV Magazine, August 22–28, 1971 (B)

60

Los Angeles Herald Examiner Feb. 3 - 9

ST. LOUIS POST-DISPATCH AUGUST 22-28

TV Magazine

LUCILLE BALL

64

TV WEEKLY

Lucy's best all-star

65. Los Angeles Herald Examiner TV Weekly, February 3–9, 1980 (B)

65

TVue Sun...
Week of Dec...

CBS-TV'S "Here's Lucy"
Monday at 9:30 P.M.
Channels 5 and 12
SEE PAGE 21

LUCILLE BALL
An Old-Fashioned
Girl at Heart

TV Sweepstakes . . . $2500 Weekly Prizes . . . See Details Inside

JACK & LUCY IN LAUGH CARNIVAL

62

62. Los Angeles Times
TV Times,
March 17–23, 1968 (B)

63. Boston Sunday
Advertiser TVue,
December 21–27,
1969 (B)

63

The Wisconsin State Journal
tv-week
Network/Cable Listings
Nov. 3-9

'Stone Pillow'

November 16-22
20¢

TV
TIME and CHANNEL

LUCY

In the midst of production for her
CBS special (Tuesday Night)
"HAPPY ANNIVERSARY and GOODBYE,"
Lucy reminisces about once
instructing Richard Burton
in the Art of Acting.

66. Lucy returned to CBS television in 1985 for a rare
dramatic performance as a bag lady living on the streets
of New York in "Stone Pillow." The Wisconsin State
Journal TV-Week showcased her in character on the
cover of their November 3–9, 1985, issue (B)

66

67. TV Time and Channel,
November 16–22,
1974 (B)

67

Television's Cover Queen ♥ **31**

"The Lucy Show": "Chris's New Year's Eve Party,"

A Comic on a Comic

In 1940 RKO Studios released *Dance, Girl, Dance,* a musical comedy that cast Lucille Ball in a not-so-typical role as a stripper at a burlesque house. For the film Lucy did a dance that not only wowed audiences but also began her career as a comic-strip character.

In those days King Features Syndicate issued a weekly comic strip called "Seein' Stars—America's Greatest Comic Weekly." Every Sunday on the pages of newspapers across the country, readers were sure to find this celebrity-related strip featuring a few of Hollywood's brightest lights in illustrated form, accompanied by captions of questionable veracity. In the August 25, 1940, installment the center of attention was Lucille Ball, illustrated in her hula attire from *Dance, Girl, Dance.* According to "Seein' Stars," the hula skirt Lucy wore in the film weighed less than a pound but consisted of more than a mile of "highly inflammable" cellophane strips!

A decade later Lucille Ball appeared for the first time on the cover of a comic book. The cover of the January 1950 issue of D.C. Comics' *Miss Beverly Hills of Hollywood* features her along with three other Hollywood stars of the time—Hedy Lamarr, Sterling Hayden, and William Bendix. Inside the issue is a three-page story titled "The Road to Stardom: Featuring Lucille Ball." It begins with a depiction of a young Lucy skipping rope with her friend and ends with a promotion for her then-current Paramount comedy, *Sorrowful Jones.*

The same story reappeared eight months later in another DC comic book, *Feature Films Presents: Fancy Pants*—the comic-book equivalent of the 1950 Lucille Ball–Bob Hope movie of the same name.

Soon after the "I Love Lucy" television series debuted the following year, everyone's favorite redhead could be seen not only on the CBS television network every Monday evening but also on the pages of daily newspapers. The first installment of the "I Love Lucy" comic strip premiered in the comics section of newspapers across the country on Monday, December 8, 1952. Written by Lawrence Nadel and drawn by Bob Oksner, the strip, which appeared at one time or another in 132 newspapers, featured typical "I Love Lucy" shenanigans every Monday through Saturday. Sunday editions carried an "I Love Lucy" strip with a slightly different twist: an endorsement for Philip Morris cigarettes was incorporated into each installment. What initially appeared to be a bona fide Sunday comic strip was actually a cleverly disguised Philip Morris advertisement.

By 1954 the antics of Lucy Ricardo, her husband Ricky, and their friends and landlords, Fred and Ethel Mertz, could also be found in the form of *I Love Lucy* comic books. Originally designed and produced by the Western Printing and Lithography Company, *I Love Lucy Comics* were published by Dell Publishing. They were issued quarterly from August 1954 through June 1962, except during May–December of 1956, when they appeared on a bimonthly basis. The original price, 10 cents, was increased to 15 in April 1961.

Over the course of the *I Love Lucy* comic books' eight-year life, thirty-five issues were produced—each featuring a photo of Lucille Ball on the cover. Desi Arnaz appears with her on several covers, but not a single cover features the likenesses of William Frawley or Vivian Vance (the Mertzes).

Another Lucy-related comic book published by Dell was issued in 1956 to coincide with the release of Lucy and Desi's third and final film together, *Forever Darling.* Like the movie, the comic book tells the story of Susan and Larry Vega's married life. The cover depicts the happy couple in wedding attire. James Mason, who costarred in the film as Susan Vega's guardian angel, is also featured.

Seven years later, in 1963, Gold Key Comics began a limited, five-issue comic-book series based on Lucy's second weekly TV program, "The Lucy Show." The covers of the first two issues feature color photos of Lucille Ball as Lucy Carmichael, the character she played on the show. The covers of the rest of the issues are illustrations—each with a black-and-white photo of Lucille Ball inset in the upper right-hand corner.

Today Lucille Ball–related comics are quite valuable on both the comic-book and Hollywood-collectibles markets. It can take a collector many years to acquire a complete set of these illustrated magazines originally intended for children.

68. "Seein' Stars" newspaper comic strip, August 25, 1940 (C/D)

69. DC Comics' *Feature Films Presents: Fancy Pants,* September–October 1950 (E)

70. Hedy Lamarr, Sterling Hayden, Lucille Ball, and William Bendix are all featured on the pages of DC Comics' *Miss Beverly Hills of Hollywood,* no. 6, January–February 1950 (C)

71

72

73

71–73. Three installments of the "I Love Lucy" Sunday comic strip, 1952 (each: C/D)

74

74–109. *I Love Lucy Comics:* published by
Dell Publishing Co.; designed and produced
by Western Printing and Lithographing Co.;
copyright © Lucille Ball and Desi Arnaz

74. *I Love Lucy Comics,*
no. 535 (first issue), 1954 (C/D)

75. *I Love Lucy Comics,*
no. 559 (second issue), 1954 (C/D)

76. *I Love Lucy Comics, no. 10,*
   May–June 1956 (B/C)

77. *I Love Lucy Comics, no. 5,*
   February–April 1955 (B/C)

78. *I Love Lucy Comics, no. 8,*
   November–January 1956 (B/C)

79. *I Love Lucy Comics*, no. 12,
September–October 1956 (B/C)

80. *I Love Lucy Comics*, no. 4,
November–January 1955 (B/C)

81. *I Love Lucy Comics*, no. 3,
August–October 1954 (C)

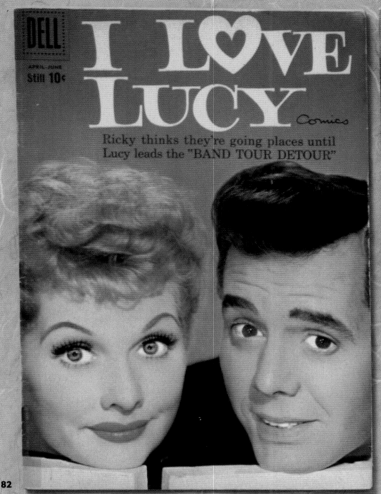

82. *I Love Lucy Comics*, no. 23, April–June 1959 (B/C)

83. *I Love Lucy Comics*, no. 22, January–March 1959 (B/C)

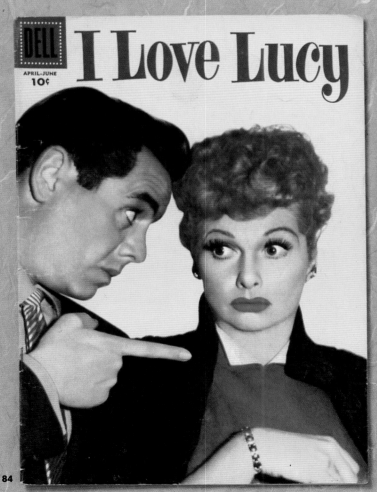

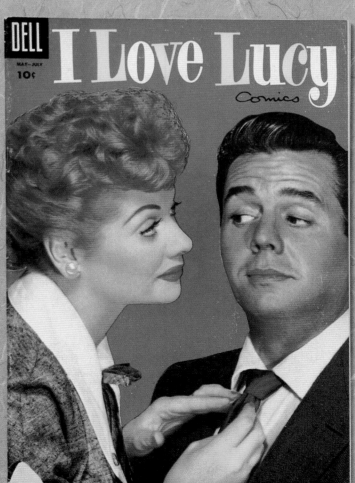

84. *I Love Lucy Comics*, no. 15, April–June 1957 (B/C)

85. *I Love Lucy Comics*, no. 6, May–July 1955 (B/C)

86. *I Love Lucy Comics*, no. 24, July–September 1959 (B/C)

87. *I Love Lucy Comics*, no. 16, July–September 1957 (B/C)

Ricky goes on the warpath when Lucy loses her new bracelet!

88. *I Love Lucy Comics*, no. 27, April–June 1960 (B/C)

89. *I Love Lucy Comics*, no. 7, August–October 1955 (B/C)

90. *I Love Lucy Comics,*
no. 19, April–June
1958 (B/C)

91. *I Love Lucy Comics,*
no. 11, July–August
1956 (B/C)

92. *I Love Lucy
Comics,* no. 13,
November–
December
1956 (B/C)

93. *I Love Lucy
Comics,* no. 9,
February–April
1956 (B/C)

94. *I Love Lucy Comics*, no. 21, October–December 1958 (B/C)

95. *I Love Lucy Comics*, no. 4, November–January 1955: interior spread

96. *I Love Lucy Comics*, no. 14, January–March 1957 (B/C)

97. *I Love Lucy Comics*, no. 20, July–September 1958 (B/C)

98

98. *I Love Lucy Comics*, no. 18,
January–March 1958 (B/C)

99. *I Love Lucy Comics*, no. 17,
October–December 1957 (B/C)

100

100. *I Love Lucy Comics,*
no. 25, October–
December 1959 (B/C)

101

102

103

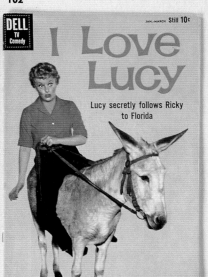

104

101. *I Love Lucy Comics,*
no. 31, April–June
1961 (B/C)

102. *I Love Lucy Comics,*
no. 28, July–September
1960 (B/C)

103. *I Love Lucy Comics,*
no. 33, October–
December 1961 (B/C)

104. *I Love Lucy Comics,*
no. 26, January–March
1960 (B/C)

105. *I Love Lucy Comics,*
no. 30, January–March
1961 (B/C)

105

106

107

108

106. *I Love Lucy Comics,*
no. 29, October–
December 1960 (B/C)

107. *I Love Lucy Comics,*
no. 34, January–March
1962 (B/C)

108. *I Love Lucy Comics,*
no. 35, April–June
1962 (B/C)

109. *I Love Lucy Comics,*
no. 32, July–September
1961 (B/C)

109

110. *The Lucy Show* comic book, no. 1, June 1963: published by K.K. Publications, Inc., in cooperation with Golden Press, Inc.; designed, produced, and printed by Western Printing and Lithographing Co.; copyright © Desilu Productions, Inc. (B/C)

111. Dell's *Forever Darling* comic book (no. 681) was copyrighted in 1956 by Zanra Productions, Inc.—that's "Arnaz" spelled backward (C)

112. *The Lucy Show* comic book, no. 2, September 1963 (B/C)

113. "Lucy and Viv bungle in the jungle" in *The Lucy Show* comic book, no. 5, June 1964, the last in the series (B/C)

114. *The Lucy Show* comic book, no. 4, March 1964, brings Lucy and Viv to a military academy in the story "T'anks But No Tanks" (B/C)

115. *The Lucy Show* comic book, no. 3, December 1963: "Still only 12¢" (B/C)

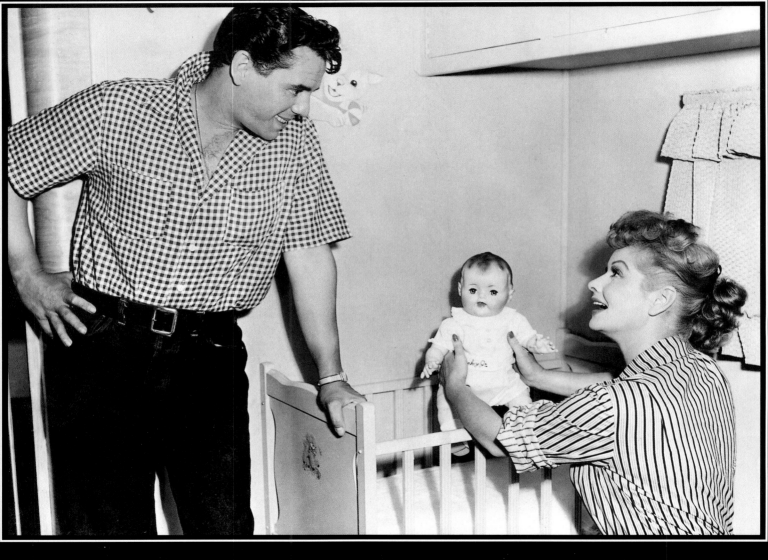

Desi and Lucy admiring a Ricky Jr. doll, c. 1954

What a Doll!

When Lucille Ball became pregnant with her second child in 1952, "I Love Lucy" was still in its first season. After careful consideration, the decision was made to incorporate the pregnancy into the show's second-season story lines—making "I Love Lucy" the first prime-time television series to address the topic of pregnancy, although the word itself could not be used on the air.

Lucille Ball's (and Lucy Ricardo's) pregnancy in 1952 generated a merchandising boom for everyone from knitting yarn companies to nursery furniture manufacturers. Numerous products were successfully marketed as tie-ins to the birth of both the Arnaz baby and the fictional Ricardo tot.

Shortly after America learned of Lucy's pregnancy, the American Character Doll company released an "I Love Lucy Baby" doll, but it wasn't available for long. On January 19, 1953, Lucille Ball gave birth twice. First, Desi Arnaz Jr. was born in a Los Angeles hospital. Later that evening, more than forty-three million people watched as the expectant Lucy Ricardo was rushed off to the delivery room on "I Love Lucy." Before the closing credits rolled up the screen, viewers got their first glimpse of Little Ricky.

As soon as the whole country knew that Lucy had had a boy, the "I Love Lucy" baby doll became obsolete and was quickly replaced by brand new Ricky Jr. dolls. Also manufactured by American Character, these Little Rickys came in a variety of styles and sizes. Some could even drink from a bottle and blow bubbles. All, however, had one thing in common—the name "Ricky Jr." embroidered on the little tyke's clothing. During the holiday season, Christmas catalogs and department stores also carried accessories for the Ricky Jr. doll, including a doll carriage and bath. Originally selling for $12.95, the doll carriage stands twenty-two inches high, and the words *Ricky Jr.* are inscribed across its sides. The Ricky Jr. doll baths feature caricatures of Lucy and Ricky Ricardo in addition to the Ricky Jr. markings. Complete with dressing table, this bath stands almost thirty inches high and was offered in the Montgomery Ward 1953 Christmas catalog for $10.95.

A Ricky Jr. layette, consisting of a two-piece Sunday suit, nursing bottle, and more, was also available. Each layette was packaged in a gift album featuring a picture of Lucy and Desi holding their own Ricky Jr. doll.

Still another Little Ricky doll was produced in 1953, this time a finger puppet by Zany Toys of Saint Louis. Complete with his own blanket, this ten-inch-tall Little Ricky comes dressed in flannel pajamas—all ready for bed. An identification tag sewn onto the blanket reads "I am Ricky Jr. © Lucille Ball and Desi Arnaz." Simply by slipping your hand underneath the blanket and inserting your fingers in the openings, you can make Little Ricky move. The puppet originally came packaged in a colorful box that pictures the proud parents holding their newborn.

Little Ricky wasn't the only "I Love Lucy" character to be represented in doll form. In fact, of all the Lucy-related dolls, none is more sought after than the 1952 Lucy Ricardo rag doll. Twenty-eight inches tall, with orange yarn hair tied up in a scarf and saucer-blue, painted-on eyes, this doll is a fun likeness of the Lucy Ricardo TV character. Today it is an incredibly rare find. The lucky collector who comes upon one should expect to pay $1,000 or more to take it home.

Introducing Lucy, the Paper Doll

Seven full years before Lucy made her appearance as a rag doll, she lent her likeness to a paper doll. In 1945, following the success of her 1943 MGM comedy *Du Barry Was a Lady*, the Saalfield company developed two similar folder sets of Lucille Ball paper dolls modeled after her role as May Daly in the film. Many of the lavish costumes she wore in the movie were adapted on paper for these "Lucille Ball Movie Star" paper-doll sets.

In 1953 three more Lucille Ball paper-doll sets were marketed, this time by Whitman Publishing. Using "I Love Lucy" as the theme, Whitman transformed Lucy and Ricky Ricardo into cardboard cutouts, complete with their own wardrobes. Two of these sets were folder sets, each selling for 25 cents. The folder of one of them opens up into a dressing room for the stars; the folder of the other has a bright yellow background, and this set includes a Little Ricky cutout. Little Ricky was also part of the third, more expensive set. Originally priced at 98 cents, this set came boxed with a ribbon tie closure.

When Lucille Ball returned to weekly television in 1962 as the star of the CBS comedy "The Lucy Show," Whitman created three new Lucy paper-doll sets. Children could make up their very own Lucy episodes with the "Lucy and Her TV Family" paper-doll set. Distributed in 1963, this 59-cent set includes not only Lucy Carmichael and her children, Chris and Jerry, but also Lucy's best friend, Vivian Bagley, and Viv's son, Sherman. The other two sets also appeared in 1963. Both feature Lucy by herself. One is a boxed set with enough clothes to keep someone's little fingers busy for hours. The other, a less expensive set, presents a more glamorous Lucille Ball in a bright magenta and white folder.

For information on recent Lucille Ball collectible dolls, see chapter 12.

117. The rare 1952 "I Love Lucy Baby" doll is 16 inches long and came complete with a drawer full of accessories and an American Character Doll company flier picturing Lucille Ball; original price: $9.98 (doll: E; doll w/box: E/F)

116. Magazine ad for the "I Love Lucy Baby" doll, c. 1952 (B)

Lucille Ball and Desi Arnaz present the fabulous "I LOVE LUCY BABY" DOLL

You will see Lucy and Desi play Poppy and Mommy with this wonderfully lifelike doll on the "I Love Lucy" T. V. Show . . . You will see Lucy feed it, diaper it, watch it cry real tears, pacify it . . . YOUR little girl too can do all these things with "I Love Lucy Baby"

she cries real tears

"I Love Lucy Baby"

She drinks, wets, bathed, CRI 16"

Lucille Ball star of the fabulous "I LOVE LUCY" T.V. show, with "I LOVE LUCY BABY"

116

117

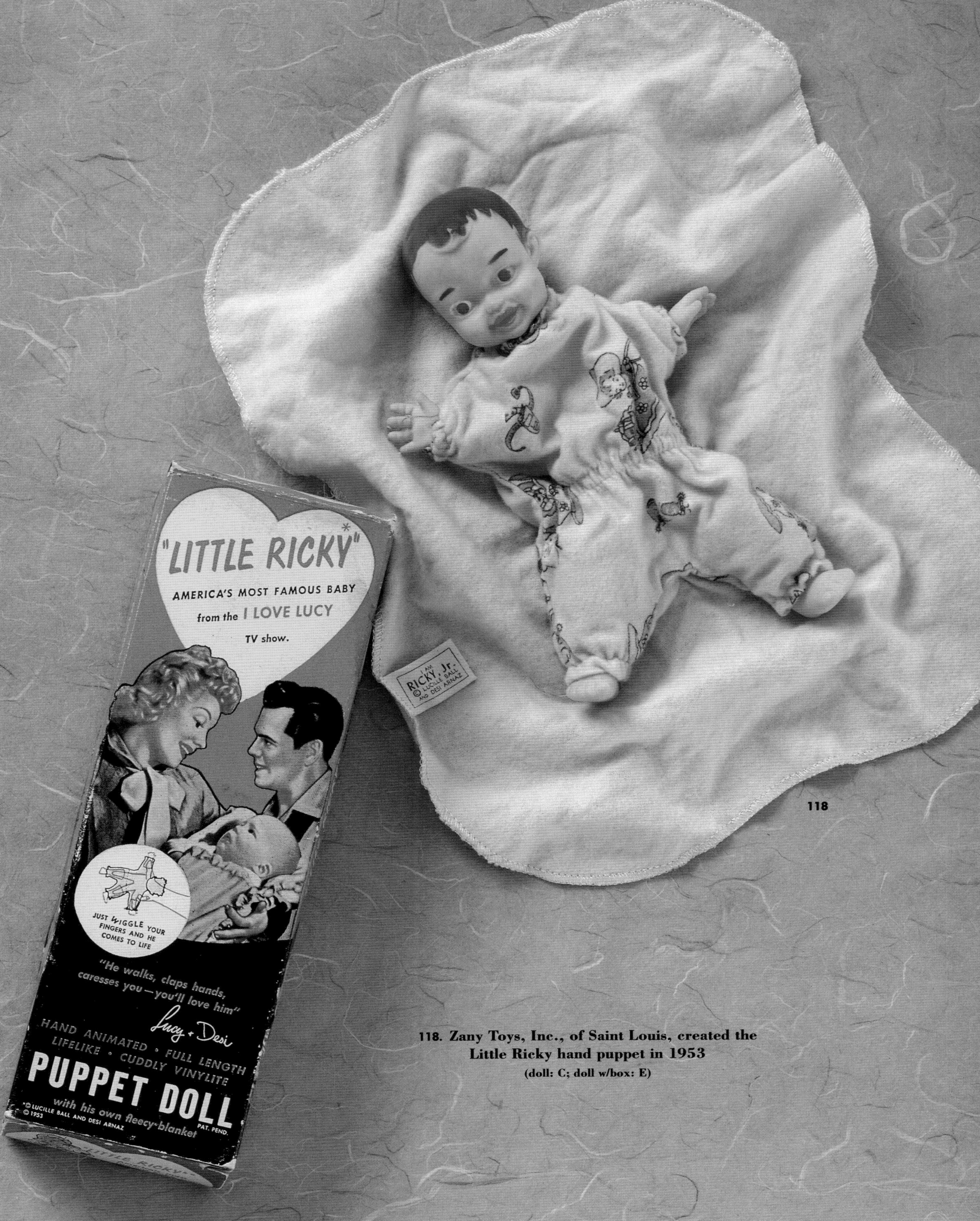
"LITTLE RICKY"*
AMERICA'S MOST FAMOUS BABY
from the I LOVE LUCY
TV show.
JUST WIGGLE YOUR FINGERS AND HE COMES TO LIFE
"He walks, claps hands, caresses you—you'll love him"
Lucy + Desi
HAND ANIMATED • FULL LENGTH
LIFELIKE • CUDDLY VINYLITE
PUPPET DOLL
with his own fleecy blanket
PAT. PEND.
*© LUCILLE BALL AND DESI ARNAZ © 1953
RICKY, Jr.
© LUCILLE BALL AND DESI ARNAZ

118

118. Zany Toys, Inc., of Saint Louis, created the Little Ricky hand puppet in 1953
(doll: C; doll w/box: E)

119

119–120. The American Character Doll company's
Ricky Jr. dolls, c. 1953, came in various sizes and
styles, including a Ricky Jr. with beanie (no. 119 [E])
and a slightly larger version (no. 120 [E])

120

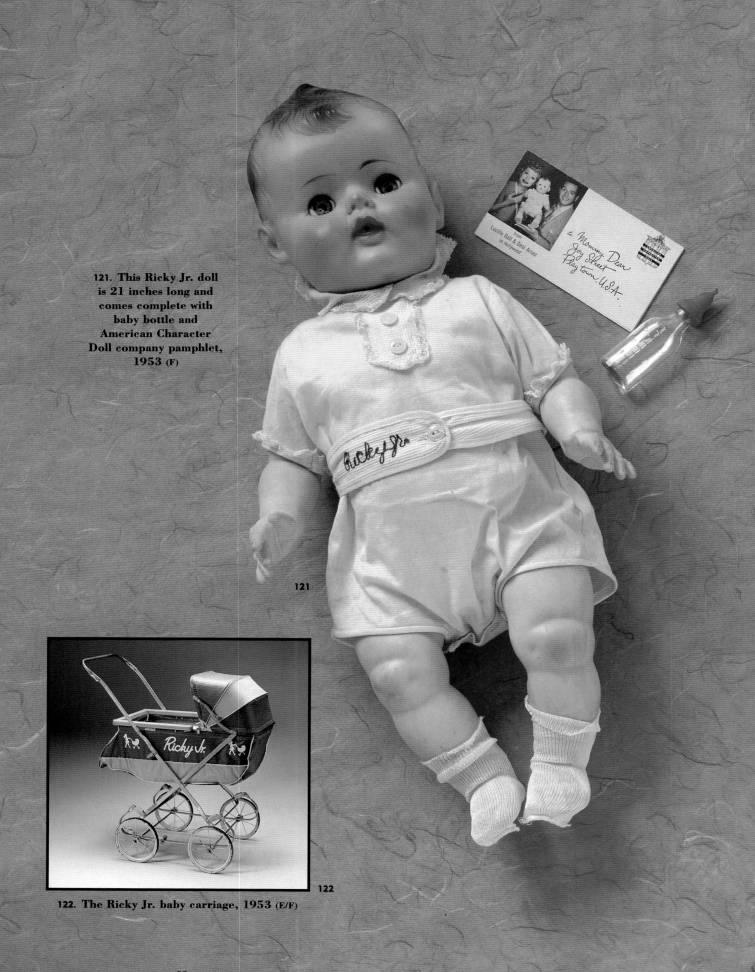

121. This Ricky Jr. doll is 21 inches long and comes complete with baby bottle and American Character Doll company pamphlet, 1953 (F)

121

122. The Ricky Jr. baby carriage, 1953 (E/F)

122

123. The rare "I Love Lucy" Lucy Ricardo rag doll, 1953 (F/G)

123

LUCILLE BALL

PAPER DOLLS

338

338
COPYRIGHT 1945 BY THE SAALFIELD PUB. CO.
AKRON, O.   MADE IN U.S.A.

A Metro-Goldwyn-Mayer Star

AUTHORIZED EDITION

124

124. The Saalfield
Publishing Company of
Akron, Ohio, produced
this authorized edition
of Lucille Ball paper
dolls, 1945 (D/E)

125. Another Saalfield
paper-doll set features
costumes worn by
Lucille Ball in the 1943
MGM musical comedy
Du Barry Was a Lady
(D/E)

Lucille Ball PAPER DOLLS

Metro-Goldwyn-Mayer Ar...

125

126. "I Love Lucy" paper-doll set, Whitman Publishing (C/D)

127. A set of Lucille Ball and Desi Arnaz "statuette dolls," Whitman Publishing, 1953 (C/D)

128. This 1953 Lucy-Desi paper-doll folder set from Whitman includes Little Ricky (C/D)

60 ♥ **What a Doll!**

129. No scissors necessary for this uncommon boxed Lucy paper-doll set from Whitman, 1963 (D)
130. "Lucy and Her TV Family" paper-doll set—another 1963 Whitman creation (C/D)
131. Lucy goes solo in this 1964 Whitman paper-doll set (C/D)

"Here's Lucy" publicity photo, c. 1973

Let's Play with Lucy

The Games Lucy Played

Throughout the 1960s, the Transogram Toy Company specialized in creating board games based on then-current television shows. "The Flintstones," "The Jetsons," "My Favorite Martian," and "Hogan's Heroes" were among the many popular shows represented in Transogram's board-game line. Another series that found itself transformed into a board game starred a redheaded widow, Lucy Carmichael, and her divorced friend Vivian Bagley. This situation comedy, simply titled "The Lucy Show," was Lucille Ball's second weekly series for CBS. Developed in 1962, "The Lucy Show" board game features black-and-white images of the cast on the box cover. Game players become either "Lucys" or "Vivians," and they all enter a contest in which the winner receives one million dollars.

"The Lucy Show" wasn't the only Lucille Ball series to be promoted through board games. In the 1970s, while "Here's Lucy" was enjoying top-ten status, the Milton Bradley company developed their own line of board games endorsed by Lucille Ball. Unlike "The Lucy Show" game, the Milton Bradley games did not rely on Lucy's television character for theme or format; they simply pictured Lucille Ball on the box lids.

In 1972 Milton Bradley marketed a tabletop billiard game called Pivot Pool, which Lucy claimed to be her "favorite family game." The following year the company released Pivot Golf. A tabletop miniature golf game, it features a color image of Lucy on the box front along with her handwritten claim that "you'll love this miniature golf game." One more Lucy-endorsed Milton Bradley game was released in 1973: a "habit-forming" card game called Solotaire.

In 1974 Lucille Ball decided to end "Here's Lucy's" six-season run and retire from the grind of weekly series television. And so, with Lucy no longer a prime-time fixture on CBS, Milton Bradley issued their last two Lucy-endorsed board games, Cross Up in 1974 and Body Language in 1975.

Another "Here's Lucy" spinoff product came from the people at View-Master in 1971. "Lucy and the Astronauts," the

October 11, 1971, episode of "Here's Lucy," was transformed into a three-reel View-Master set. Complete with storybook, this children's picture-disk toy told the tale of how a redheaded housewife found herself quarantined with three astronauts.

Color Her Red

Years before the Lucy board games were introduced to America's younger generation, children had already become accustomed to playing with Lucy. During the "I Love Lucy" days she had been a popular paper doll, and several different Lucy coloring books also kept youngsters occupied.

Whitman Publishing created two oversize coloring books in the 1950s, each featuring a photograph of Lucille Ball and Desi Arnaz on the cover. The interior illustrations depict typical "I Love Lucy" situations, the ideas for which were often based on scenes from the show. For example, Lucy can be found playing a saxophone, taking dance lessons, selling a vitamin tonic, and even giving Ricky hair treatments.

Another "I Love Lucy" coloring book was produced in 1955. Published by Dell, this one includes Little Ricky on the cover and throughout the uncolored pages. And in 1959 Golden Press offered a 29-cent "I Love Lucy" activity book featuring "the adventures of Lucy and Ricky—with pictures to trace, color, and cut out."

In 1962, after starring in *Wildcat* on Broadway, Lucy began work on "The Lucy Show." Once again, a coloring book was developed as a merchandising tie-in to the series. On the pages of this Golden Press book you'll find Lucy, Vivian, and the kids waiting for their clothes and surroundings to be filled with color.

"The Lucy Show" was also the subject of a hardcover children's storybook. In *Lucy and the Madcap Mystery*, the "Lucy Show" cast goes camping and runs into bad weather and some uninvited guests.

These children's books occasionally turn up on the antiques and collectibles markets. When located, however, they are usually in worn, secondhand condition.

Chapter 4

132. Transogram's 1962
The Lucy Show Game
features photographs of
the series' stars on the
box lid (D/E)

132

133. Pivot Golf from Milton Bradley, 1973, about which Lucy says, "You'll love this miniature golf game. I broke par— can you?" (C)

134. Pivot Pool, the first Milton Bradley game endorsed by Lucille Ball, 1972 (C)

135. Milton Bradley's Body Language, Lucy's party pantomime word game, 1975 (B)

136. Milton Bradley's Solotaire, 1973, came with a warning from Lucy: "Caution: this game may be habit forming!" (B)

137. Cross Up, believed to be the last Milton Bradley game endorsed by Lucy, 1974; note the original price, $4.39, stamped on the box lid (B)

137

138. The "Here's Lucy" episode "Lucy and the Astronauts" was captured on this hard-to-find View-Master three-disc set, complete with storybook, copyright © Lucille Ball Productions, Inc., 1971 (C)

138

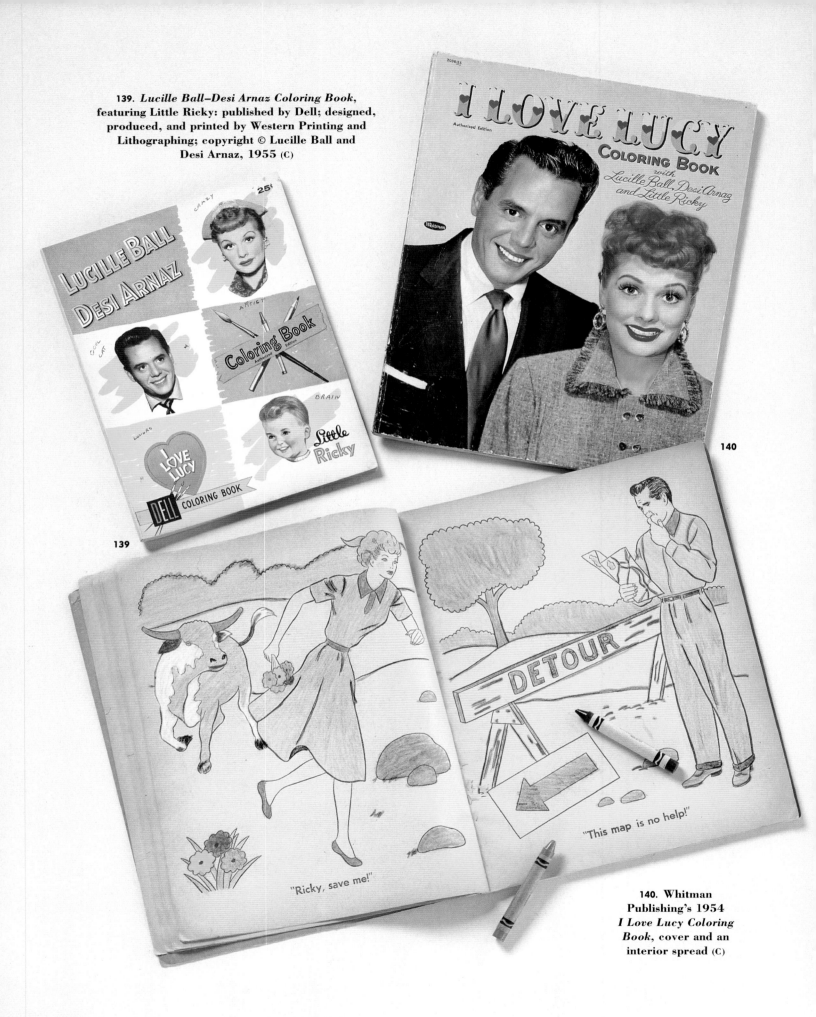

139. *Lucille Ball–Desi Arnaz Coloring Book,* featuring Little Ricky: published by Dell; designed, produced, and printed by Western Printing and Lithographing; copyright © Lucille Ball and Desi Arnaz, 1955 (C)

139

140

"Ricky, save me!"

"This map is no help!"

140. Whitman Publishing's 1954 *I Love Lucy Coloring Book,* **cover and an interior spread** (C)

141. *Lucy and the Madcap Mystery,* a hardcover children's storybook published by Whitman, 1963 (B)

142. *The Lucy Show Cut-Out Coloring Book:* copyright © Desilu Productions, 1963 (C)

143. *Lucille Ball–Desi Arnaz Coloring Book:* published by Whitman Publishing Co., copyright © Lucille Ball and Desi Arnaz, 1953 (C)

144. *I Love Lucy* tracing book: published by Golden Press, Inc.; printed by Western Printing and Lithographing Co.; copyright © Desilu Productions, Inc., 1959 (C)

Forever Darling, MGM, 1956

Lucy Goes to the Movies

orever will she be our First Lady of Comedy—America's grand dame of television. But for years before becoming a permanent fixture on the small screen, Lucille Ball had focused her attention on achieving stardom on the big screen. The Lucille Ball who appeared in the movies was often very different from her television counterpart.

She was a mean bitch as Gloria Lyons in *The Big Street* and a not-so-modest showgirl when tackling the burlesque circuit in *Dance, Girl, Dance*. As Gwendolyn Dilley in *I Dream Too Much*, her sassy side shone through. And during the filming of *Lured* for United Artists, she found herself stalked by a killer.

She was a restaurant owner, a lion tamer, a harem girl, and a nightclub singer. She sold real estate, served jail time, and survived a plane crash in the jungles of South America. And before she clowned with the Marx Brothers, Lucille played football with the Three Stooges.

Having appeared in more than seventy films before finding her home in television, Lucille Ball had become known as "Queen of the B Movies." For all her efforts at the studios, none of her films earned her Motion Picture Academy recognition. The legacy of her movie career is a collection of often-forgotten films documented by a plethora of publicity material that has been given a second life within the collectibles world.

Movie posters designed to herald the release of the studio's latest attempt to capture an audience were developed in a variety of different sizes to best meet the publicity demands of individual theaters. The most common of all movie posters is known as the one sheet, still the standard format for film publicity today. Among Lucille Ball admirers, one sheets from *Too Many Girls*, *The Long, Long Trailer*, and *Forever Darling* are favorites, as these three films also starred Desi Arnaz.

Other types of movie posters include inserts, which are long and narrow, and smaller-size lobby cards. As a rule, a set of eight lobby cards was produced for each movie. The first card in the set is the "title" card, often featuring elaborate graphics. Each of the other seven cards depicts a different scene from the film. For example, lobby cards from Lucy's 1950 comedy *The Fuller Brush Girl*, showing her misadventures as that unpredictable door-to-door saleswoman (see page 76), serve as an enticing preview to the film.

Movie press books served as a visual guide to these promotional film materials. Flipping through the pages of a movie press book, theater managers could see at a glance all available movie poster styles and sizes, publicity stills, press releases, cast biographies, merchandising tie-ins, and other promotion suggestions for the film.

A 1954 press book for *The Long, Long Trailer*, Lucy and Desi's second film together, provides a catalog of available movie posters, movie stills, and press releases. It also offers clever ideas on how to develop a giveaway contest for New Moon Trailer Homes—the brand of mobile home used in the film.

In 1960, to coincide with the release of Lucille Ball and Bob Hope's third film together, *The Facts of Life*, a novelization of the movie was published in a paperback edition by Perma Books, complete with the stars' images on the cover.

When Lucille Ball returned to the big screen in 1974 to play the title role in Warner Brothers' *Mame*, publicity tie-ins, such as wall mirrors and ashtrays bearing the *Mame* graphics (see page 161), were produced to help promote her homecoming and generate interest in the film.

Originally not intended to fall into the hands of the general public, vintage movie memorabilia continues to show strong investment potential and enjoys increasing popularity.

Movie Poster Lingo

Lobby cards (11 × 14″): Small movie posters, usually produced in sets of eight: one "title" card and seven different "scene" cards. Title cards typically feature the artwork and graphics found on larger posters and can command higher prices than scene cards. ♥ **Window cards** (14 × 22″): Small movie posters printed on heavy poster paper and featuring a blank border that was used by individual theaters to insert show times and theater information. These cards were intended to be displayed in the windows of local businesses to advertise a film's arrival to the area. ♥ **Display cards** (22 × 28″): Often hung in theater lobbies, these posters served as a final preview of a film. Also known as half sheets. ♥ **Inserts** (14 × 36″): Uniquely sized, these long, narrow posters were usually printed on durable stock and often contain detailed graphics. ♥ **One sheets** (27 × 41″): The standard and most commonly collected movie poster, usually printed on thin paper. ♥ **Three sheets** (41 × 81″): Three times larger than one sheets. Because of their large size, three sheets are generally less desirable collectibles than one sheets. ♥ **Six sheets** (81 × 81″): Six times larger than the standard movie poster, and quite impressive. ♥ **Twenty-four sheets:** Billboard-size posters. ♥ **Press books:** Publicity booklets containing a film's promotional materials and usually picturing all available posters and stills related to the film. Also known as campaign books. ♥ **Movie stills** (8 × 10″): Glossy publicity photographs of the stars and major scenes of a film, often with production and copyright information.

Chapter 5

146. As this magazine ad for MGM's *The Long, Long Trailer* states, the film is "the first appearance on the big, big movie screen and in color of America's most mirthful married couple," 1954 (A/B)

CELEBRATING M·G·M's 30TH ANNIVERSARY

M·G·M SCOOP!

...nouncing the first ...pearance on the big, big ...vie screen **and in color** ...merica's most mirthful ...ried couple! ... first picture together ...they became the ...'s love-and-laugh ...ites! And what a ...erful story! It thrilled ...s as a best-seller ...Reader's Digest!

Lucille Ball and Desi Arnaz "The Long, Long Trailer"

WITH MARJORIE MAIN · KEENAN WYNN
ALBERT HACKETT and FRANCES GOODRICH · CLINTON TWISS
Directed by VINCENTE MINNELLI · Produced by PANDRO S. BERMAN An M·G·M Picture

146

145. *The Long, Long Trailer* one- sheet movie poster, 1954 (D)

145

147. *Forever Darling* one
sheet, 1956 (C/D)

148. *Miss Grant Takes
Richmond* display card,
1949 (C)

149. *Her Husband's
Affairs* insert, 1947 (C/D)

150. This 1946 press book for MGM's *Ziegfeld Follies of 1946* features an artist's rendering of Lucille Ball on the cover (C)

151. The 1954 MGM press book for Lucy and Desi's most memorable film together, *The Long, Long Trailer* (C/D)

152. A publicity still for *The Long, Long Trailer*, MGM, 1963 reissue (A)

153. The 1950 press book for *The Fuller Brush Girl* touts Lucille Ball as "much, much prettier than 'The Fuller Brush Man'" (C)

74

154–63. Publicity stills from various Lucille Ball films (each: A)

154. *Lover Come Back,*
Universal, 1946
155. *Forever Darling,*
MGM, 1956
156. *The Fuller Brush Girl,*
Columbia, 1950
157. *Fancy Pants,*
Paramount, 1950
158. *Her Husband's Affairs,*
Columbia, 1947
159. *Her Husband's Affairs,*
Columbia, 1947
160. *Lured,* United
Artists, 1947
161. *Personal Column,*
United Artists, 1947
162. *Personal Column,*
United Artists, 1947
163. *Without Love,*
MGM, 1945.

164 165

164–67. Lobby cards from Columbia's 1950 comedy *The Fuller Brush Girl*, including the title card (no. 166) and three scene cards

(each: C)

166 167

168 169

170 171

168–73. Lobby cards from MGM's 1956 Lucy-Desi film, *Forever Darling*, are perennially popular with fans. Costar James Mason can be found on one of the scene cards (no. 170) and the title card (no. 173) (each: B)

172 173

174

175

176

177

178

179

180

181

182

183

174–83. Lobby cards from a variety of Lucille Ball's movies

174. *Beauty for the Asking*, RKO, 1939 (C)

175. *Lover Come Back*, Universal, 1952 reissue (B)

176. *Easy to Wed*, MGM, 1946 (B)

177. *Look Who's Laughing*, RKO, 1952 reissue (B)

178–79. *Mame*, Warner Brothers, 1974 (each: B)

180. *The Long, Long Trailer*, MGM, 1954 (C)

181. *Personal Column*, United Artists, 1947 (C)

182. *Yours, Mine and Ours*, United Artists, 1968 (B)

183. *The Dark Corner*, 20th Century Fox, 1946 (C)

184–85. Lobby cards from Lucille Ball and Bob Hope's fourth and final film together, *Critic's Choice*, 1963 (each: B)

184

185

186. *Critic's Choice* one sheet, Warner Brothers, 1963 (B/C)

186

187

187. Window card from the comedy *Sorrowful Jones*, Paramount, 1949 (C)

188. Lobby card from *Sorrowful Jones*, 1949 (C)

189. Lobby card from *Fancy Pants*, Paramount, 1950 (C)

188

189

190. A 1961 one sheet from *The Facts of Life*, United Artists, 1960 (B/C)

191–92. Lobby cards from *The Facts of Life*: title card (no. 191) and a scene card (no. 192)

(each: B)

And Now, a Word from Our Sponsor

The Lucy Endorsement

The celebrity endorsement has remained one of the most popular advertising strategies for the past fifty years. Leafing through an old *Life* magazine, you can spot many top Hollywood stars promoting everything from hand cream to carpeting—and the feisty redhead with the big blue eyes was no exception.

Lucille Ball product endorsement ads have been traced back as far as the early 1940s, when she lent her name to products as diverse as gelatin and shoe polish! As one of the stars of MGM's *Ziegfeld Follies* in 1946, Lucille Ball told magazines readers "what a wonderful discovery" Max Factor's Pan-Cake Make-Up was. That same year she proclaimed that "RC [Cola] tastes best" in magazine ads and cardboard window signs.

While starring in the CBS radio series "My Favorite Husband" (1948–51), Lucille Ball promoted Carling's Red Cap Ale, endorsed Hoover vacuum cleaners, and recommended La France laundry detergent via magazine advertisements.

During the original run of "I Love Lucy," Lucy and Desi could be found pitching everything from pajamas to casement windows. But undoubtedly their most notable endorsement was for Philip Morris cigarettes, the original sponsor of the show. Having secured Philip Morris as sponsor, the stars of "I Love Lucy" lent their likenesses to the cigarette company and soon found themselves pictured in full-page magazine advertisements, shelf talkers, display signs, and even "Lucy's Notebook," a Philip Morris premium booklet containing Lucy's party tips and favorite recipes.

In a clever merchandising campaign during the 1952 and 1953 Christmas seasons, Philip Morris designed holiday cigarette cartons featuring Christmas scenes with Lucy and Desi. Because these cartons had no real value at the time, most were tossed away. Today these cigarette cartons picturing the famous couple are rare finds.

Lucy And Dixie

Philip Morris wasn't the first company to take celebrity endorsements beyond the bounds of magazine ads. Several years earlier, Lucille Ball could even be found in your grocer's freezer!

Throughout the 1940s and 1950s, the Dixie company packaged small ice cream treats in paper containers known as Dixie cups. And today, some fifty years later, the cardboard lids of these frozen desserts have become popular collectibles.

Why would anyone collect ice cream lids? The answer is surprisingly simple. The underside of each Dixie-cup lid pictured a then-current movie star promoting his or her latest film. You never knew who was lying face down in your ice cream until you peeled back the lid and gave it a lick. Clark Gable, Bob Hope, Judy Garland, Ginger Rogers, and yes, Lucille Ball were among the dozens of stars to be included in this clever marketing gimmick.

The Dixie-cup lid campaign proved successful, owing in part to the development of a premium offer. Once twelve lids had been collected, they could be returned to the distributor in exchange for a full-color, scrapbook-style movie star photo. A brief biography of the featured star appeared on the reverse of the photo.

Lucille Ball was featured twice on Dixie-cup lids. First, in 1941, she was pictured in character as the star of the RKO comedy *A Girl, a Guy, and a Gob*. Ten years later, with the rise of television, Dixie-cup lids began featuring TV personalities in addition to movie stars. And in 1953 a lick of the lid might have revealed Lucy with husband Desi Arnaz.

You, Too, Can Live Like Lucy

The secret was out. Soon other companies began watching profits soar as "I Love Lucy" merchandising tie-ins were developed left and right. A furniture company created desks and occasional tables modeled after those seen on the sitcom, while the Johnson-Carper Furniture Company told readers, "You, too, can live like Lucy," in magazine ads promoting their line of "I Love Lucy" bedroom suites. There were even Lucy-inspired floor coverings from the Sloane-Delaware Company. Sloane's 1953 "Floor Planning For Your 'I Love Lucy' Home" catalog not only provides color samples of its vinyl tiles and linoleum but also tells the story of how Lucy turned her house into "something better than a place to hang your hat."

For the mother-to-be, there were Ricky Jr. knitting yarns (Bernat), infant bathtubs (Trimble, Inc.), baby clothes (McKem Vanta), mattress and crib pads (Rose-Derry Co.), insulated diaper bags (Alexander Miner Manufacturing Corp.), and potty chairs (Moulded Products)—each carrying the "I Love Lucy" endorsement.

There never were any officially licensed Lucy lunch boxes, wastebaskets, baseball bats, or bicycles. But Lucille Ball's image could often be found on such items, thanks to the Meyercord Company of Chicago, which produced full-color Star-cal decals featuring portraits of many Hollywood stars, including Lucy. With a quick dip in warm water, a Lucille Ball decal could easily be applied to almost any clean surface. And presto, a Lucy lunch box was born.

For the women of the 1950s, Weber Originals marketed "I Love Lucy" blouses, and Suzy Boutique found its niche selling "I Love Lucy" sweaters. Housewives could be seen in the kitchen wearing Gingham Girl's "I Love Lucy" aprons while their husbands went to work wearing "I Love Lucy" zippered jackets (Ethan Ames) and "I Love Lucy" dress shirts (Lion of Troy). For a more casual look, Desi Denims, as well as Desi smoking jackets and bathrobes (Dunmar), were just a department store away. And who could forget the matching pajamas Lucy and Ricky Ricardo wore on the show? Any fine clothing store was sure to have these "his and her" pajamas (Harwood) in stock for the suggested retail price of $6.95 a pair.

If your budget wouldn't allow the luxury of these trendy fashions, the Advance pattern company offered a less expensive alternative with their line of Lucy and Ricky clothing patterns. Collectors today search high and low for these unusual forms of Lucille Ball nostalgia.

In 1959, as a tie-in to the "Lucy Goes to Alaska" episode of the "Lucy-Desi Comedy Hour," the show's sponsor, Westinghouse Electric, published the "Pocket Encyclopedia of Alaska, the 49th State." Complete with a map of the new state, its population statistics, and information on its national parks, this brochure features illustrations of Lucy and Desi on the cover, indirectly suggesting that Westinghouse was the famous couple's preferred brand of household appliances.

"Carousel Cookery," a holiday recipe booklet from Lucy, Desi, and Westinghouse, was available during the 1959 Christmas season. The cover depicts the famous couple dressed in Santa suits and enjoying a ride on a reindeer carousel atop a two-layer frosted cake.

Lucy Loves Lucite . . . and More

After Desi Arnaz and Lucille Ball parted in 1960, Desi stepped away from center stage but continued producing new programs

Lucille Ball, as photographed by Mead-Maddick, on the set of "I Love Lucy" (Monday Nights, CBS-TV).

"I love telegrams," says Lucy—"especially Bunnygrams!"

Television's one and only Lucy is reading a Bunnygram to little Ricky. It's Western Union's special Easter greeting for children. Don't you know a child who would be as thrilled as Ricky to get his own Easter telegram, signed by Peter Rabbit himself? Of course you do! Call Western Union today!

And when you do, don't forget the grownups. Be sure to send *them* the Easter greeting that says so much . . . the *personal* message on Western Union's beautifully decorated Easter greeting blank. Share your joy with family and friends the most thoughtful way of all—Easter greetings by wire.

Lucy reads a Western Union Bunnygram to Little Ricky, 1957 (B; see also no. 252, page 99)

"Lucy's Notebook!" 1950s
(C; see also no. 246, page 98)

for Desilu. Lucy went on to star in two more television series before retiring from the small screen in 1974. And Lucille Ball product endorsements continued as well.

If Lucy were asked, "Where can a mother find the answers to her children's questions?" chances are she would have replied, "Encyclopaedia Britannica, of course!" After her divorce Lucille Ball served as a spokesperson for the encyclopedia in magazine ads. She also appeared on boxes of Pepsodent toothpaste, offering "Lucille Ball's Special: Save 6¢" as part of a Lever Brothers sales campaign.

Whenever Lucy decided to repaint her home—inside or out—you can bet she chose DuPont's Lucite paints. In the 1960s DuPont brochures, cardboard table signs, and other advertising paraphernalia for their line of house paints pictured Lucille Ball. "Lucy loves Lucite" was the claim. Today, some thirty years later, collectors love Lucy loving Lucite. Those who took Lucy's "expert" advice and painted their walls with Lucite paint were also likely to have heeded her recommendation to cover their floors with Royalweve carpets.

Ice cream, cigarettes, carpeting, and toothpaste. Soda, encyclopedias, pajamas, and house paint. Lucille Ball's power to influence America's buying habits is but one indication of how deeply loved and trusted she was.

193. Lucy "leads the cheering" for the apple, celery, and grape salad recipe found in this 1940 Royal Gelatin magazine ad (A)

195. Lucy and Desi lent their likenesses to Westinghouse's "Carousel Cookery" booklet of festive holiday recipes, 1950s (C)

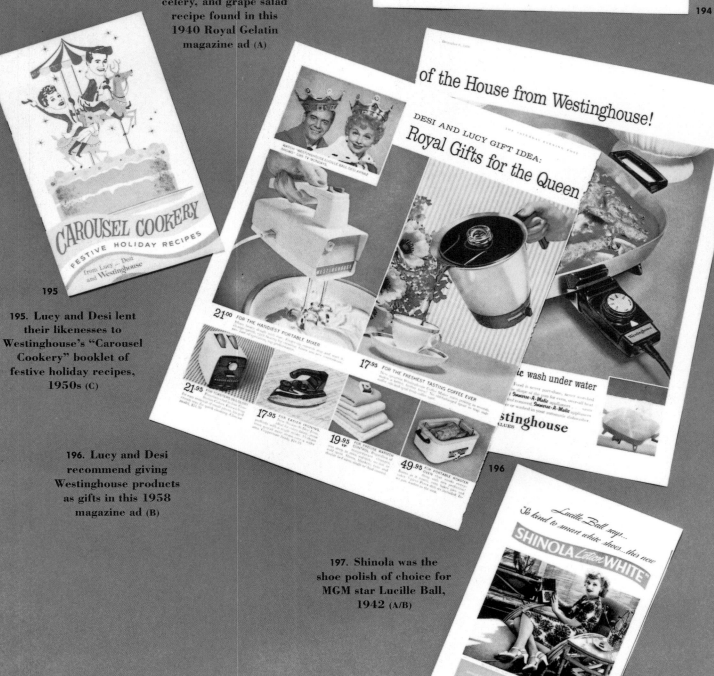

196. Lucy and Desi recommend giving Westinghouse products as gifts in this 1958 magazine ad (B)

197. Shinola was the shoe polish of choice for MGM star Lucille Ball, 1942 (A/B)

198. In this 1949 magazine ad, Lucy claims,
"Chesterfields are completely satisfying" (A)

199. A good cigarette deserves a good lighter,
and in 1949 Lucy's choice was ASR (A)

200. Roma Wines won
Lucy's endorsement
in this 1948
advertisement (A)

201. Roma Wine Coolers
also met with Lucy's
approval, 1948 (B)

202

202–3. Philip Morris cigarettes ran a number of Lucy-Desi magazine ads such as these throughout the early 1950s (each: A)

204. This two-page Philip Morris magazine ad ran in 1953 (B)

203

204

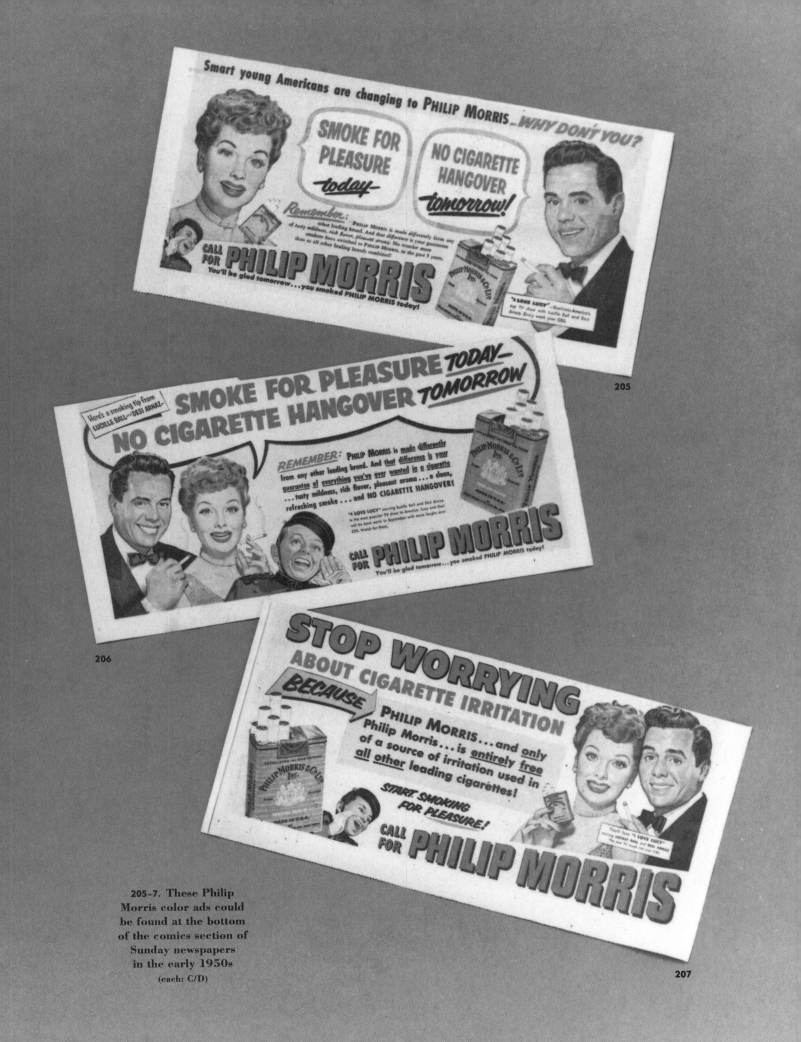

205–7. These Philip
Morris color ads could
be found at the bottom
of the comics section of
Sunday newspapers
in the early 1950s
(each: C/D)

208. Lucy and Desi
celebrate Father's Day
on this rare Philip
Morris shelf talker,
early 1950s (E)

208

209

209. Why not take a
suggestion from Lucy?
Give cartons of Philip
Morris cigarettes for
Father's Day, 1953 (A/B)

210. A full-page
magazine ad picturing
Philip Morris's
1952 Christmas
carton (B)

210

211. A 1952 newspaper ad entices readers to give Philip Morris cigarettes for Christmas (C/D)

212. Philip Morris's 1953 Christmas carton is hard to locate in any condition (D/E)

213. This full-color magazine ad, which originally appeared in the *Saturday Evening Post*, pictures the 1953 Christmas carton (B)

214. Lucy does the "tissue test" for Woodbury Cold Cream in this black-and-white magazine ad, 1951 (A)

215–17. A glamorous Lucille Ball did her best to promote other Woodbury beauty products in these magazine ads from the 1940s (each: A/B)

218. Buy Max Factor Pan-Cake Make-Up and you, too, can be as gorgeous as Lucille Ball, a 1940s ad suggests (A)

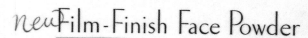

214

215

216

217

218

219-20. Nursery products, as seen on "I Love Lucy," made their way onto the market in 1953 (each: A)

220

221. According to this Jergens Lotion ad, the hands of Lucille Ball are "de-licious" and "de-lovely," 1940s (A)

222. During the run of *Lured*, Lucy promoted Max Factor lipstick, 1947 (B)

223. For Lucy, the place to find answers to her children's questions was on the pages of Encyclopaedia Britannica, 1966 (B)

219

221

222

223

224. In 1950 Hoover signed the redhead to endorse their aero-dyne vacuum cleaners (B)

225–26. General Electric frequently pictured Lucy and Desi on the screens of their Ultra-Vision televisions in magazine ads, early 1950s (each: A)

227. Lucy makes waffles for K-M Appliances in this 1949 ad (A)

228. Lucy pictured with a look-alike drew readers' attention to this Auto-Lite car battery ad, 1949 (A)

229. New Moon, the manufacturer of the mobile home featured in Lucy and Desi's 1954 film *The Long, Long Trailer*, took advantage of the tie-in in their ads (A)

230. This late 1950s ad implies that if Lucy and Desi drive a Henry J, it must be a special car (A)

231. Wearing a Monsanto "I Love
Lucy" raincoat, you'll "laugh at
the weather"—just as you laugh
at the show, 1950s (B)

231

232

232. "You won't have to 'run for
cover' when the doorbell rings"
if you wear "I Love Lucy"
pajamas by Harwood, 1950s (B)

233. Lucy promoted Summerette
shoes as "the star of Paramount's
forthcoming hit, *Sorrowful
Jones*," 1949 (B)

233

234. Before becoming TV's Lucy, Lucille Ball was a familiar face on movie screens. Here, her image is used to endorse a now-rare Hollywood Pattern, 1940s (C/D)

236. Readers of *Woman's Home Companion* found this full-color ad for Advance's Lucy and Ricky bathrobe patterns in the December 1954 issue (B)

235, 237. In 1954 the Advance pattern company sold clothing patterns modeled after the Ricardos' TV attire. Among the patterns available were: Lucy's robe, Desi's robe (no. 235), Lucy's apron (no. 237), and Desi's apron (each: C)

235

236

237

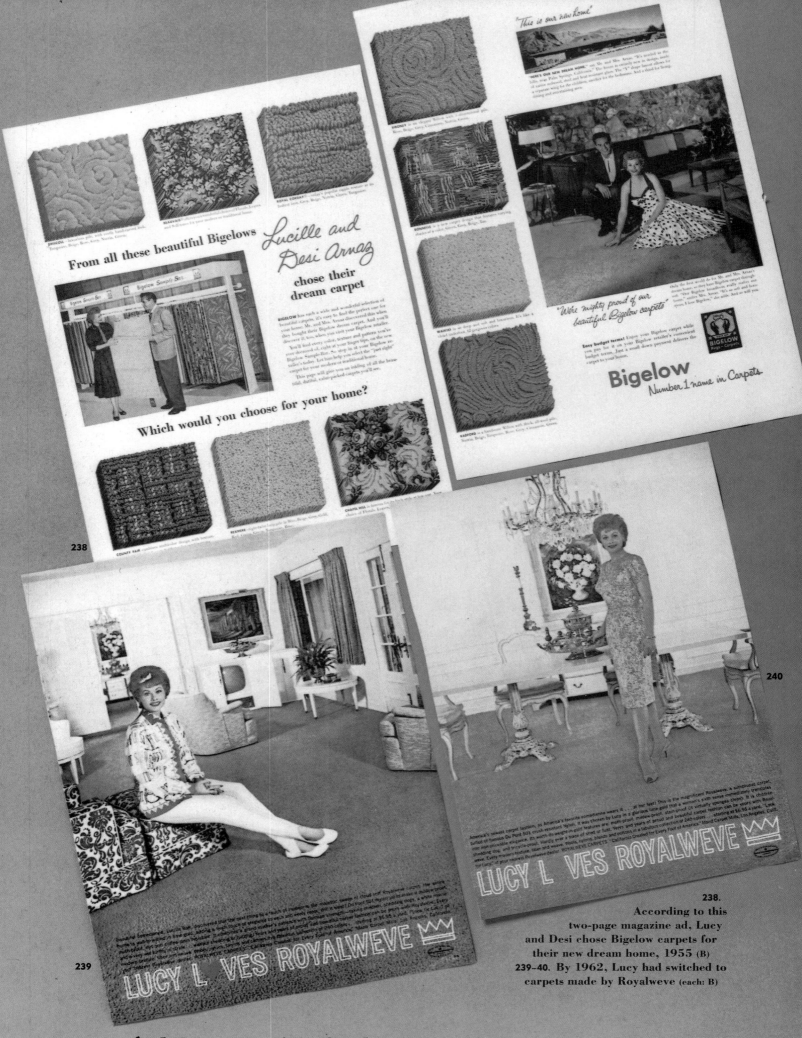

238.
According to this
two-page magazine ad, Lucy
and Desi chose Bigelow carpets for
their new dream home, 1955 (B)
239-40. By 1962, Lucy had switched to
carpets made by Royalweve (each: B)

241–42. For their "magnificent Desi Arnaz Western Hills Hotel" the couple preferred Allen Rubber-Loc carpet padding, 1957 (each: A)

243. In 1955 the comedy duo even promoted swing doors and casement windows (A)

241

242

243

244

244. Schumacher's asked Desi Arnaz to pitch the uniqueness of the company's fabrics, carpets, and wallpapers in this half-page ad, which first appeared in *Better Homes and Gardens*, 1956 (A)

245

245. In this 1950s ad for Morgan-Jones Minuet bedspreads Lucille Ball asks readers, "Can you imagine a more beautiful bedspread?" (A)

246. The cover and an interior spread of "Lucy's Notebook!"— a 44-page booklet containing recipes, entertaining tips, and other secrets from the star of "I Love Lucy," 1950s (C)

LUCILLE BALL, too, has graduated to Carling's—the LIGHT-HEARTED ale!

Lucille Ball stars in the CBS radio series, "My Favorite Husband."

CANADA'S GREAT ALE IS NOW BREWED IN U.S.A.!

© 1951
Brewing Corporation of America
Cleveland, Ohio

CARLING'S *Red Cap* ALE

Brewed *light* in the U.S.A. to suit American tastes... Carling's Red Cap Ale has lost none of the gusto and *heart* of its proud Canadian heritage. And bright, clear, *light-hearted* Carling's— so uniquely *right* for light-hearted moments —costs no more than fine premium beer!

Why don't *you* graduate to *light-hearted* Carling's...today?

247

LUX TOILET SOAP Bath Size

NOW—Hollyw... in new

Lucille L...

248

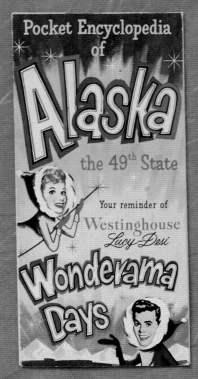

250–51. Lucille Ball
Star-cal decals by the
Meyercord Co.,
mid-1940s (each: B/C)

250

249. In 1959 Westinghouse published the
"Pocket Encyclopedia of Alaska, the 49th
State," as a reminder of the "Westinghouse
Lucy-Desi Wonderama Days" (B/C)

249

251

OF LEVER BROTHERS COMPANY

Beauty Soap
SIZE

beauty bath
, so luxurious,"
s this famous star

e Lux Soap is wonderful,"
cille Ball. "It makes my
more delightful than ever."
y tip from one of Hollywood's
e generous, satin-smooth
et Soap. The creamy lather
and dirt, leaves skin really
perfumed, too, with a lovely
ce that clings!

Paramount Pictures'
FUL JONES"

Lucille Ball, as photographed by Mead-Maddick, on the set of "I Love Lucy" (Monday Nights, CBS-TV).

"I love telegrams," says Lucy—"especially Bunnygrams!"

Television's one and only Lucy is reading a Bunnygram to little Ricky. It's Western
Union's special Easter greeting for children. Don't you know a child who would be
as thrilled as Ricky to get his own Easter telegram, signed by Peter Rabbit himself?
Of course you do! Call Western Union today!

And when you do, don't forget the grownups. Be sure to send *them* the Easter
greeting that says so much . . . the *personal* message on Western Union's beautifully
decorated Easter greeting blank. Share your joy with family and friends the most
thoughtful way of all—Easter greetings by wire.

BUNNYGRAMS FOR
CHILDREN . . .
EASTER WIRES FOR
GROWNUPS!

BY WESTERN UNION

252

247. The redheaded star
of the CBS radio series
"My Favorite Husband"
was a natural choice
as a spokesperson for
Carling's Red Cap Ale,
1951 (B)

248. Lever Brothers
counted on readers to
take a beauty tip from
"one of Hollywood's
loveliest stars" and
try bath-size Lux Toilet
Soap, 1949 (B)

252. Lucy reads
a Western Union
Bunnygram to Little
Ricky, 1957 (B)

253. This 1943 Dixie-cup lid features Lucille Ball as she appeared in *A Girl, a Guy, and a Gob* (B/C)

254. This 1943 Dixie-cup premium photo is the full-size version of the image on the Dixie-cup lid. The reverse provides a brief biography of Lucy and stills from her latest film (C/D)

LUCILLE BALL
R.K.O. Star
IN ACTION

This little lady is the living incarnation of Vivacity! Her mother a concert pianist, it was expected that music would be her field, but Lucille pined for the stage, enrolled in a dramatic school, and landed in Ziegfeld's "Rio Rita" as showgirl. Then a modelling position, posing for national advertisers, then to Hollywood with a group of famous poster girls for "Roman Scandals"! That was in '35. The others have gone. But this talented reddish-blonde with the winning smile and sparkling blue eyes, is attaining top-flight stardom!

She's fond of sports of all kinds, loves flying and believe it or not . . . she's an avid reader of biographies!

255. A portrait of Lucy and Desi could be found on select Dixie-cup lids in 1953 (B/C)

Lucille Ball— Desi Arnaz

STARS OF THE PHILIP MORRIS "I LOVE L[...] TELEVISION SHOW

The most excitingly popular people on [...] today are Lucille Ball and Desi Arnaz [...] the top comedy series, "I Love Lucy." [...] Ricardos, they play a young married co[...] whom a steady stream of amusing things h[...] almost the same as in real life.

Ever since Lucille Ball was born in Jamesto[...] New York, the unexpected has happened to her[...] At 15 she entered dramatic school, and even [...] though she was told she would never become an [...] actress, she wasn't discouraged. Soon a talent [...] scout discovered her and sent her to Hollywood, [...] where she made many pictures. While working [...] in the movie "Too Many Girls," she met Desi [...] Arnaz, who was to become her husband.

Born in Cuba, Desi Arnaz came to the United [...] States with his mother in 1933. He worked at all [...] sorts of jobs before playing a guitar in a 7-piece [...] rhumba band. Later he joined Xavier Cugat, and [...] gathered so many fans that he organized [...]own [...] band. Then Desi went to Hollywood [...] leading lady was beautiful Lucille B[...] still his leading lady both in real l[...] "I Love Lucy."

Don't miss a week[...] "I LOVE LUCY[...] America's top tele[...] entertainment, prod[...] Desilu Productio[...]

"The second-hand dealer agrees to sell the furniture back to Ricky."

"Ricky lets Lucy get in on a jam session."

"Lucy winds up with a black eye."

"Ricky, Fred and Ethel flatter Lucy out of her inferiority complex."

Save Any 12 Dixie Picture Lids For A Large Picture Of Us
See Your Dealer For Inform[...]

LUCILLE BALL AND DESI ARNAZ
Stars of the Fabulous Philip Morris
"I Love Lucy" Show
CBS-TV TELEVISION STARS

255

256

Dixie
WILSON'S
MELLO-PAK
CHOCOLATE
ICE CREAM

256. Anyone who mailed in twelve Dixie-cup lids could receive this premium scrapbook photo, which features scenes from "I Love Lucy's" second season on the reverse (C/D)

Lucille Ball—Desi Arnaz

258. Thanks to Lucy, consumers could save 6¢ on this tube of Pepsodent toothpaste, 1965 (E)

257. In this 1946 magazine ad for Royal Crown Cola, Lucy suggests that a day at the beach wouldn't be complete without RC Cola (B)

259. On this 11 × 28″ window-display sign, Lucy and RC make a winning combination, 1940s (D/E)

260. As this rare tabletop DuPont paint display sign attests, Lucite loved Lucy, c. 1963 (E)

261. "Love that Lucite" DuPont paint brochure, c. 1963 (D)

262. With Lucy and Desi's authorization, Sloane-Delaware produced this floor-planning catalog in 1953 (D)

"I Love Lucy": "Job Switching,"
originally broadcast September 15, 1952

Lucy's Got It Covered

The Early Years

In March 1938, a twenty-six-year-old brunette was showcased in black and white on the cover of *Radio Guide*, an oversize weekly magazine that was then a popular source for radio program schedules. At the time, Lucille Ball could be heard every Sunday night on CBS radio's "Phil Baker Show."

Similar magazines soon followed *Radio Guide*'s lead. *Radio News and Short Wave*, a 25-cents-an-issue magazine providing information on everything from home-built transmitters to power-pack rectifiers, saluted Miss Ball with a full-color photo on the cover of its April 1938 issue. Although the cover identified her merely as "Phil Baker's heckler," a short cover story buried inside the magazine informed readers that she was an actress named Lucille Ball.

In the early days of her movie career, the young actress appeared on the cover of some unlikely publications. *The Billboard*—a magazine that touted itself as "the world's foremost amusement weekly" and was chock-full of entertainment ideas, carnival dates, and classified ads for out-of-work jugglers—chose Lucille Ball for the cover of its July 2, 1938, issue. Readers of *Barber's Journal*—a men's barbershop magazine—expecting to see the latest designs in razors and learn the distinct differences between a facial and a massage, must have been pleasantly surprised to find a certain redheaded beauty on the cover of the March 1942 issue.

A Rising Star in the Spotlight

But as the 1940s progressed, Lucille Ball's star in the Hollywood firmament shone ever brighter. Cast in film after film opposite such leading men as Victor Mature, Henry Fonda, Red Skelton, Bob Hope, and William Holden, she became one of the big screen's most recognizable actresses. Throughout the decade she could frequently be found on the covers of *Screen Romances*, *Movie Life*, *Movie Show*, *Screenland*, and many other movie magazines, portrayed with all the glamour and beauty she projected on the screen. Her celebrity status, however, had not yet begun to reach its peak.

Lucy—TV's Favorite Funny Lady

In the early 1950s, when television was in its infancy, Lucille Ball left the movies and her hit radio series, "My Favorite Husband," to pursue a project for the new medium. The comedy series she and husband Desi Arnaz created and starred in remains the most successful in television history. Within a few short weeks of its premiere, "I Love Lucy" had tickled the funny bones of millions of Americans. TV watchers became so caught up in the madcap adventures of Lucy and Ricky Ricardo and their neighbors Fred and Ethel Mertz that they began planning their week around their Monday evening visits with their new friends on East Sixty-eighth Street.

Lucy quickly became a popular cover subject for the new television theme magazines, including *TV Stage*, *TV Life*, *TV World*, *TV and Movie Screen*, and *TV Spotlight*, all of which did their best to showcase the zany lady with the flaming red hair. While some articles focused on the off-screen details of her marriage to that dashing Cuban singer and bongo player, others analyzed her overwhelming appeal with the American public.

America's Love for Lucy

Television magazines weren't the only periodicals to highlight TV's brightest star on their pages. *Cosmopolitan* magazine explained why "20,000,000 fans watch Lucille Ball slapstick her way to stardom" in its January 1953 issue. *Family Circle* caught up with Lucy and Desi at work at the MGM studios during the filming of *The Long, Long Trailer* and provided readers with a pictorial preview of the movie in its September 1953 issue. *Guideposts* and *Adult Psychology* both tackled the subject of the survival of the celebrity marriage, whereas a 1968 issue of *Lady's Circle* gave Lucy the chance to reminisce about Christmases past.

In April 1953, several months after Desi Arnaz Jr. was born, both *Look* and *Life* devoted cover stories to the Arnaz family. Throughout the 1950s Lucy also proved to be a popular choice for the covers of the pocket-size publications *People Today*, *Quick*, and *Tempo*.

For those interested in the latest Hollywood gossip, *Police Gazette*, *Whisper*, and *Down Beat* splashed the "private wars of Lucy and Desi" all over their covers. Readers wanting more credible reporting could turn to *Time* or *Newsweek* and still not miss out on the Lucy phenomenon.

In the Papers

Yet another category of periodical that loved to feature Lucy on the cover was the supplement magazine, found among the sections of the Sunday newspaper. *The Sunday Mirror*, *Family Weekly*, *Grafic Magazine*, and *Parade* are only a few of the many supplements that celebrated Lucy over the years. Of course, most of these supplements suffered the same fate as the newspapers in which they were found; after being read, they were unceremoniously tossed in the trash. So those that survived are highly prized by collectors.

Chapter 7

263. One of Lucille Ball's first magazine covers was this issue of *Radio Guide* for the week ending March 5, 1938 (D)

264. *Radio News and Short Wave*, April 1938 (D)

266. *Barber's Journal,*
March 1942 (C/D)

266

265. *The Billboard,*
July 2, 1938 (D)

265

267–81. Sunday newspaper supplements captured the many looks of Lucy

267. *Chicago Sunday Tribune Picture Section,* **January 5, 1947** (B/C)

268. *New York Sunday Mirror Magazine Section,* **July 18, 1943** (B/C)

269. *Sunday News: New York's Picture Newspaper,* **September 22, 1946** (B/C)

270. *Sunday News: New York's Picture Newspaper,* **April 19, 1942** (B/C)

271. *Sunday News: New York's Picture Newspaper,* **August 27, 1950** (B/C)

272. *Sunday News: New York's Picture Newspaper,* **April 2, 1944** (B/C)

273. *New York Sunday Mirror Magazine Section,* **October 1, 1950** (B/C)

274. *New York Sunday Mirror Magazine Section*, October 19, 1952 (B/C)

275. *New York Mirror Magazine*, October 27, 1957 (B/C)

276. *Chicago Sunday Tribune Grafic Magazine*, April 26, 1953 (B/C)

277. *Waterloo Daily Courier Family Weekly*, February 12, 1956 (B/C)

278. *Chicago Sunday Tribune Picture Section*, March 8, 1953 (B/C)

279. *New York News Coloroto Magazine*, January 18, 1959 (B/C)

280. *New York Sunday Mirror Magazine Section*, April 12, 1953 (B/C)

281. *Sunday News: New York's Picture Newspaper*, February 27, 1955 (B/C)

NEWS WEEKLY · APRIL 13, 1953 **10¢**

Quick

REPORT ON
Southeast
Asia

$8,000,000
BABY
Lucy &
Desi IV

282

282. *Quick,*
April 13, 1953 (B/C)

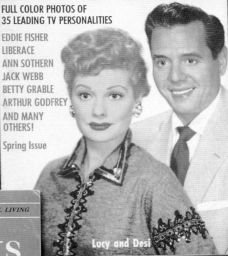

COLOR PORTRAITS OF YOUR FAVORITE STARS **ANC 25¢**

TV STARS

**FULL COLOR PHOTOS OF
35 LEADING TV PERSONALITIES**

EDDIE FISHER
LIBERACE
ANN SOTHERN
JACK WEBB
BETTY GRABLE
ARTHUR GODFREY
AND MANY
OTHERS!

Spring Issue

Lucy and Desi

283

283. *TV Stars,*
Spring 1955 (B/C)

MAY 1954   A PRACTICAL GUIDE TO SUCCESSFUL LIVING

Guideposts

Our second wedding . . .
by LUCILLE BALL

THE day I walked
down the aisle as
Mrs. Desi Arnaz, to
become Mrs. Arnaz
again—a June bride
this time complete
with prayer book, veil
and shaking knees—
I couldn't help look-
ing back over the
steps that led us
slowly from
(see page 2)

RELIGION ROOMS
ON THE CAMPUS
A special, nationwide report
by Hartzell Spence, beginning
on page fourteen.

Also in this issue:
"Is it important to be polite?"
"The girl who wouldn't smile."
"Dear Judge: Thank you for fining me."

284

284. *Guideposts,*
May 1954 (B/C)

285. *Quick,*
October 13, 1952 (B/C)

286. *Quick,*
November 27, 1950 (B/C)

NEWS WEEKLY · OCT. 13, 1952

Quick

LUCILLE BALL
& DESI ARNAZ

Why do They
Love Lucy?

285

NEWS WEEKLY · NOV. 27, 1950 **10¢**

Quick

LUCILLE BALL:
Love Is Her
Favorite
Career

CAN WE WIN THE PROPAGANDA WAR?

286

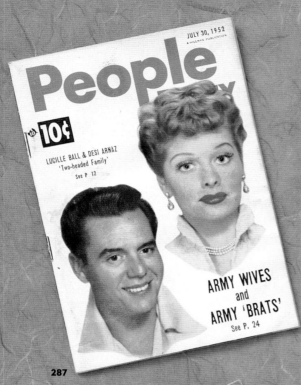

287

288

287. *People Today,*
July 30, 1952 (B/C)

288. *TV Spotlight,*
September 1953 (C/D)

289

289. *Tempo,*
November 30, 1953
(B/C)

290. *People Today,*
January 30, 1952 (B/C)

290

291. *Pic,*
October 24, 1944 (C)

292. *Movie Show,*
August 1944 (C)

293. *Movie Show,*
November 1943 (C)

294. *Movie Life,*
March 1944 (C)

295. *Movies,*
November 1944 (C)

296. *Personal Romances,*
September 1941 (C)

297. *Screenland,*
September 1944 (C)

298. *True Story,*
February 1941 (C)

299. *Movie Life,*
June 1942 (C)

300. *Screen Romances,*
May 1944 (C)

301. *Silver Screen,*
September 1943 (C)

302. *TV Stage*, April 1954 (B/C)

303. *TV Stage*, December 1956 (B/C)

304. *TV Radio Life*,
November 10–16, 1956 (C)

305. *TV Radio Life*,
September 27–October 3, 1958 (C)

306. *TV World,*
June 1955 (B/C)

307. *TV World,*
June 1956 (B/C)

308. *TV World,*
October 1953 (B/C)

309. *TV World,*
June 1953 (B/C)

310. *Who's Who in TV &*
Radio, no. 3, 1953 (B/C)

311. *Western Family,*
July 1958 (C)

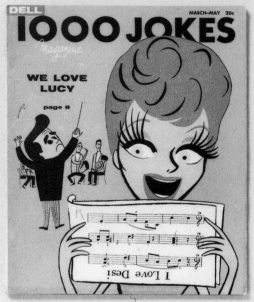

312. *1000 Jokes,*
June–August 1959 (B)

313. *1000 Jokes,*
March–May 1957 (B)

314. *Magazine Digest,*
October 1952 (C)

315. *Adult Psychology,*
no. 3, June–July 1954 (C)

316. *The Philadelphia Inquirer Colorama,* January 24, 1954 (C)

317. *TV Star Parade,* July 1955 (B/C)

318. *TV Star Parade,* April 1954 (B/C)

319. *TV Star Parade,* September 1954 (B/C)

320. *TV Star Parade,* July 1953 (B/C)

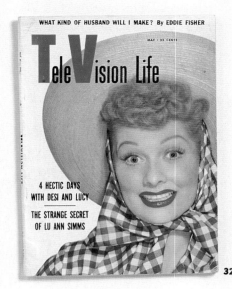

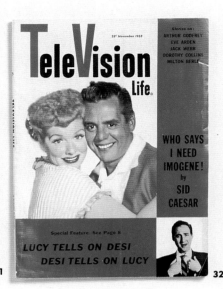

321. *TeleVision Life,*
May 1954 (B/C)

322. *TeleVision Life,*
November 1953 (B/C)

323. *TV-Radio Annual,*
1954 (B/C)

324. Lucy shares the cover of
the June 1953 issue of *TV Fan*
with Arthur Godfrey (B/C)

325. *TV and Movie Screen,*
November 1954 (B/C)

326. *TV Picture Yearbook,*
no. 1, 1954 (B/C)

327. *Tele-Views,*
March 1953 (B/C)

328. *Motion Picture and Television
Magazine,* **May 1954** (B/C)

329. *TV and Movie Screen,*
January 1954 (B/C)

330. *TV Headliner,*
November 1953 (B/C)

331. *TV Starland,*
September 1953 (B/C)

332. *TV Show,*
September 1952 (C)

333. *TV Show,*
March 1953 (C)

334. The star of
"My Favorite Husband"
made the cover of *Radio
and Television Mirror*'s
April 1950 issue (B/C)

335. *TV Illustrated,*
June 1956 (B)

336. *Palm Springs Villager*, November 1954 (C/D)

337. *Police Gazette*, March 1960 (C)

338. *Whisper*, August 1956 (B/C)

339. *Down Beat*, May 6, 1953 (B/C)

340

340. *Springfield News-Sun Parade,* September 11, 1960 (B/C)

341

342

341. *Camera 35,* October 1979 (B)

342. *Parade,* November 21, 1971 (B/C)

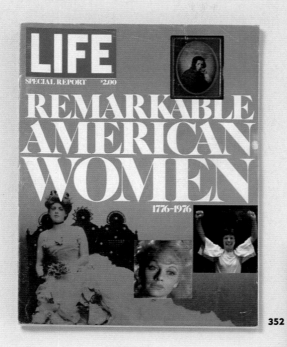

352

352. *Life Special Report,*
"Remarkable American
Women, 1776–1976,"
1976 (B)

353. *Life,*
January 5, 1962 (B)

354. *Life,*
April 6, 1953 (B)

353

354

343. *Look,*
November 18, 1952 (B)

344. *Look,*
December 28, 1954 (B)

345. *Look,*
September 27, 1960 (B)

346. *Look,*
September 17, 1957 (B)

347. *Look,*
December 25, 1956 (B)

348. *Look,*
June 3, 1952 (B)

349. *Look,*
October 9, 1962 (B)

350. *Look,*
April 21, 1953 (B)

351. *Look,*
September 7, 1971 (B)

358. *Films in Review,*
June–July 1971 (B)

355. *TV Picture Life,*
November 1966 (B)

356. *Modern Screen,*
February 1969 (B)

357. *TV Star Parade,*
June 1968 (A/B)

359. *TV Radio Mirror,*
April 1963 (B)

360. *TV Star Parade,* May 1965 (B)

361. *TV Radio Talk,*
July 1970 (A/B)

362. *Photoplay,* March 1975 (B)

363. *TV Radio Mirror,*
June 1971 (A/B)

364. *TV Radio Mirror,*
August 1971 (A/B)

371. *Films in Review,*
April 1974 (B)

365

366

367

365. *Screen Stories,*
July 1972 (A/B)

366. *Movie World,* July 1974 (A)

367. *Rona Barrett's Gossip,*
February 1976 (B)

368

369

370

368. *Rona Barrett's Hollywood,*
April 1978 (B)

369. *Rona Barrett's*
Hollywood Super Special,
Summer 1976 (B)

370. *Hollywood Studio*
Magazine, August 1981 (A/B)

372

371

373

374

372. *Hollywood Studio*
Magazine Then & Now,
July 1989 (A/B)

373. *Hollywood Studio Magazine*
Then and Now!,
November 1985 (A/B)

374. *Hollywood Then & Now,*
March 1991 (A/B)

375

375. *Time*, May 26, 1952 (C)

376

376. *Newsweek*, January 19, 1953 (C)

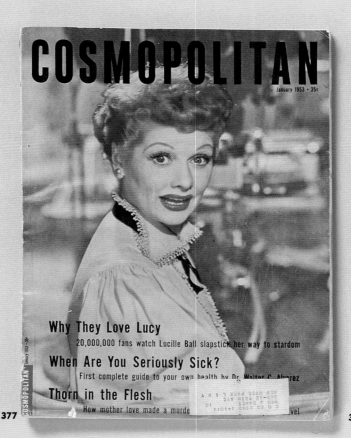

377

377. *Cosmopolitan*, January 1953 (C)

378

378. In the January 1960 issue of *Cosmopolitan*
Lucy revealed her "serious life with Desi Arnaz";
four months later they were divorced (B/C)

379

379. *Family Circle*, September 1953 (B/C)

380

380. *Lady's Circle*, January 1968 (B/C)

381

381. *Lady's Circle*, December 1968 (B/C)

"Here's Lucy": "Lucy Goes Hawaiian, Part 2,"

Lyrical Lucy

Lucille's Musical Moments

She sang off-key, played in an all-nun band, and performed "Glow Worm" on her saxophone. She wrote an operetta, directed a Christmas choir, impersonated Carmen Miranda, and sang a duet with Dinah Shore on a ski lift. She conducted the Manhattan Symphony, sang a jingle as a pickle, and coached Sammy Davis, Jr. And that was just on television.

In the movies, well before she found her home on television, she often sang or danced her way through scenes with the likes of Bob Hope, Henry Fonda, Maureen O'Hara, and Red Skelton. These musical moments often proved to be the highlights of the films, and moviegoers would rush to music stores to buy the music and lyrics to the song they had left the theater humming. It wasn't even necessary to remember the title because the stars of the film were usually pictured on the cover of the sheet music. Today this sheet music is a popular form of memorabilia, as are song-lyric magazines such as *Hit Parader* and *Big Song Magazine*, which provided the lyrics to some of Lucille Ball's most memorable movie tunes.

Desi Belts "Babalu"

While Lucy reigned as queen of the B movies, the real musical talent in her life was hard at work making a name for himself in the music world. As early as 1939 Desi Arnaz could be heard on Columbia Records singing "South American Way." And throughout the 1940s he popularized such tunes as "The Peanut Vendor," "The Matador," and his trademark hit, "Babalu." By the time he and his wife became America's favorite television couple, Desi had an impressive collection of recordings to his credit on three record labels: Decca, RCA Victor, and Columbia.

In January 1953, well into the show's second season, Columbia Records released the "I Love Lucy" theme song. The flip side featured "There's a Brand New Baby (At Our House)," a song composed in 1951 by Desi Arnaz with Eddie Maxwell, commemorating the birth of the Arnazes' daughter, Lucie. Television viewers first became familiar with the tune after Desilu incorporated it into an "I Love Lucy" episode devoted to the newborn Ricardo baby, Little Ricky.

Three years later, the redhead and the Cuban tenor filmed *Forever Darling* for big screen audiences. The title song was released on the MGM record label. The corresponding sheet music pictured Lucy, Desi, and their costar, James Mason.

They're Playing Her Song

In 1961 Lucille Ball took the Broadway stage by storm in *Wildcat*. RCA Victor produced the original-cast album of the show. For some, the *Wildcat* recording served as a vehicle to relive that Broadway experience. For others, it proved to be an inexpensive way to own a part of Broadway history.

In 1974, after starring in nearly five hundred TV episodes, Lucille Ball retired from series television. That same year she returned to the big screen in *Mame*—a Warner Brothers movie spun from the hit play by the same name, which in turn was based on the book *Auntie Mame* by Patrick Dennis. As Mame Dennis, Lucille Ball found herself roaring through the twenties, overcoming the Depression, surviving tragedy, and kicking up her heels in many musical numbers.

Mame was expected to be a major box office hit. And to promote its release in the spring of 1974, Warner Brothers distributed a special promotional soundtrack album during the 1973 Christmas season. The front cover of the album pictures Lucille Ball wearing a Santa Claus stocking cap. The back features a handwritten note from Lucy, wishing fans a "joyous holiday season . . . see you at Easter with *Mame*." Upon the film's release Warner Brothers issued the *Mame* soundtrack album nationwide. On it, Lucille's booming, full-throttle voice can be heard singing such favorites as "We Need a Little Christmas," "If He Walked into My Life," and "Bosom Buddies" with costar Bea Arthur.

Wildcat and *Mame* are only two of the Lucy-related recordings that collectors search for. Other record albums pay tribute to her earlier film work, including the soundtracks from *The Ziegfeld Follies*, *Thousands Cheer*, and *Yours, Mine and Ours*.

Every aspect of Lucille Ball's long and varied career has been documented on recordings through the years (more recent recordings are discussed in chapter 12). Although not always easily accessible, when uncovered this musical memorabilia captures some of the highlights of her work on radio, television, stage, and screen.

382. *Big Song Magazine, June 1944* (B/C)
384. *Hit Parader, April 1953* (B/C)

383. *Big Song Magazine, October 1943* (B/C)
385. *Song Hits, February 1944* (B/C)

386. *Latin American Hit Songs*, a compilation of words and music published by Capitol Stories, Inc., 1949 (B)

388. This boxed set of 45's includes "Peanut Vendor," "Cuban Pete," and Desi's trademark hit, "Babalu," 1950s (C)

389. "El Cumbanchero" sheet music, 1943 (B)

391. "In Santiago, Chile ('T'ain't Chilly at All)" sheet music, 1948 (B)

387. "Cuban Pete" sheet music, 1946 (B)

390. Probably the most sought-after of all Desi Arnaz 78's is this 1953 Columbia recording of the "I Love Lucy" theme song (C)

LSO-1060
LIVING STEREO
AN ORIGINAL CAST RECORDING
RCA VICTOR

MICHAEL KIDD and N. RICHARD NASH present

Lucille Ball in Wildcat

A New Musical by N. RICHARD NASH

Music by CY COLEMAN   Lyrics by CAROLYN LEIGH

and starring KEITH ANDES

with EDITH   PAULA   CLIFFORD   DON   HOWARD   SWEN
KING   STEWART   DAVID   TOMKINS   FISCHER   SWENSON

Settings Designed by PETER LARKIN
Costumes by ALVIN COLT
Lighting by CHARLES ELSON

Musical Direction, Dance & Vocal Arrangements by JOHN MORRIS
Arrangements & Orchestrations by ROBERT GINZLER & SID RAMIN

Entire Production Directed and Choreographed by
MICHAEL KIDD

392

TITANIA 509
ORIGINAL PRODUCTION SERIES

LUCILLE BALL
Du Barry Was A Lady

394

ORIGINAL MOTION PICTURE SOUNDTRACK
MCA Klassic SOUNDTRACKS

Yours, Mine and OURS

Composed & Conducted by FRED KARLIN

395

CURTAIN CALLS

MGM's Ziegfeld Follies of 1946

starring
FRED ASTAIRE   LUCILLE BALL
LUCILLE BREMER   FANNY BRICE
JUDY GARLAND   KATHRYN GRAYSON
LENA HORNE   GENE KELLY
JAMES MELTON   VICTOR MOORE
RED SKELTON   ESTHER WILLIAMS

and WILLIAM POWELL

with
EDWARD ARNOLD   MARION BELL
LUCILLE'S PUPPETS   CYD CHARISSE
HUME CRONYN   WILLIAM FRAWLEY
ROBERT LEWIS   VIRGINIA O'BRIEN   KEENAN WYNN

396

393

392. The original-cast recording of *Wildcat*, RCA Victor, 1961 (B)

393. "Vocal Selections from *Wildcat*," 1960: interior spread (B)

394. *Du Barry Was a Lady*, Titania Original Production Series, 1970s (A)

395. *Yours, Mine and Ours*, original motion picture soundtrack, MCA Classics Soundtracks, 1986 (A)

396. *MGM's Ziegfeld Follies of 1946*, original soundtrack recording, Curtain Calls Records, 1970s (A/B)

NEVER BEFORE ON LP ANYWHERE IN THE WORLD

LEE-BEE DISCS

BING CROSBY'S REDHEADS
LUCILLE BALL AND SPIKE JONES

SPECS SJ 101

BING & LUCY

397

ORIGINAL MOTION PICTURE SOUND TRACK

THOUSANDS CHEER

30 BIG STARS!
3 GREAT BANDS!

398

ORIGINAL SOUNDTRACK FROM THE MOTION PICTURE

LUCY
MAME

399

LOVING YOU

LUCY
MAME

400

401

397. *Bing Crosby's Redheads: Lucille Ball and Spike Jones,* Lee-Bee Discs, Ontario, 1970s (A)

398. *Thousands Cheer,* original motion picture soundtrack, Hollywood Soundstage Records (note Lucille Ball caricature in upper right-hand corner), 1970s (A)

399. *Mame,* original soundtrack, Warner Brothers Records, 1974 (B)

400. As Mame Dennis, Lucille Ball is in high spirits on the cover of the sheet music for "Loving You," 1974 (B)

401. This promotional *Mame* soundtrack recording was unavailable to the general public, Warner Brothers Records, 1973 (C)

402. "Cha-Cha-Cha" sheet music, 1954 (B)

403. Sheet music for the title song from the film *Forever Darling,* 1955 (B)

404. "There's a Brand New Baby (At Our House)" sheet music, 1953 (C)

405. "You're Nearer" sheet music from the film *Too Many Girls,* 1940 (B)

406. "There's a Brand New Baby (At Our House)" appears on the flip side of the "I Love Lucy" theme song, Columbia Records, 1953 (C)

407. "Buckle Down, Winsocki" sheet music, 1941 (B)

408. Sheet music for the title song from *The Facts Of Life,* 1960 (B)

409. Sheet music for "Gonna Fall in Love with You," from the MGM film *Easy To Wed,* 1945 (A/B)

410.
"Say That We're
Sweethearts
Again"
sheet music,
1944 (B)

411. "Love" sheet
music, 1945 (B)

410

411

412. "Havin' a
Wonderful Wish
(Time You Were
Here)," sheet
music, 1949 (B)

413. "Come
Closer To Me"
sheet music,
1945 (B)

414. Sheet music
for "Home
Cookin'," a song
from the 1950
Paramount music
al *Fancy Pants* (B)

415. The British
sheet music for
"Buckle Down,
Winsocki,"
1941 (B)

412

413

414

415

"I Love Lucy": "Desert Island,"
originally broadcast November 26, 1956

Lucy in Another Land

Maybe it was her red-hot hair that attracted foreign audiences to her. Maybe it was her glamour and charm. Or maybe it was the side-splitting way she wrapped chocolates, stomped grapes, and carried a tune. Whatever the reason, Lucille Ball was undeniably a star with universal appeal. Her television shows have been dubbed into several languages and still continue to be part of television programming far beyond America's borders. Her movies drew crowds to theaters around the globe. A unique assemblage of mementos attests to this worldwide adoration for the lady with the bow-shaped lips.

There are Australian movie posters for the 1956 Lucille Ball–Desi Arnaz film *Forever Darling* that have distinctly different looks from their American counterparts. In Mexican theaters, lobby cards for the same film enticed viewers to see *Mi pesadilla es un angel*.

Other Spanish-language lobby cards advertise Lucille Ball's *The Magic Carpet* as *La alfombra magica*, and in Belgium, Lucille Ball and Bob Hope's 1963 film *Critic's Choice* was rendered as *Ma Femme est sans critique*.

At one time, British music shops stocked the sheet music for the songs from some of Lucille Ball's films, including two of the movies she made with Bob Hope, *Sorrowful Jones* and *Fancy Pants*. The covers of this sheet music feature images of both stars.

The sheet music for the song "In Times Like These" from Lucille Ball and Dick Powell's 1944 film *Meet The People* was also published in Britain, as was "I Didn't Know What Time It Was" from *Too Many Girls*, the film that brought Lucy and Desi together.

The British movie magazine *Picturegoer*, which claimed to provide the latest information on the stars and studios of the motion picture world, featured several exquisite sepia-toned cover portraits of Lucille Ball in the 1940s. These magazines are some of the most desirable of all foreign Lucy nostalgia and often prove difficult to locate.

Hollywood magazine, the Italian counterpart of *Picturegoer*, also devoted several covers to Miss Ball. In 1937 she was featured holding a lookalike doll on the cover of France's *Mon Copain*. *Negro y blanco labores*, a Mexican women's magazine, showcased Lucille Ball on the cover of the May 1947 issue. And in Belgium, *Piccolo* magazine promoted *The Long, Long Trailer* with a color cover shot of Lucy and Desi in 1954.

Scotland, Holland, Spain, and Canada are among the countries that once distributed movie-star trading cards. These cards feature color portraits of the big-name stars of the 1940s and 1950s and often provide minibiographies on the back. Lucy is pictured on one as she appeared in the 1950 comedy *The Fuller Brush Girl;* on another she's clad in the harem attire she wore in *The Magic Carpet*. There are also trading cards showcasing Lucille Ball and Desi Arnaz as the stars of "I Love Lucy." Unfortunately, many of these cards bear no copyright or company markings, making it quite difficult to determine their age and country of origin.

Of all the international Lucy memorabilia, perhaps the most unusual are the Stompkop cigar bands, thought to be of Belgian origin. A set of twenty-four orange-and-gold cigar bands was issued, each featuring a tiny color image of Lucille Ball and company. Some picture scenes from "The Lucy Show"; others commemorate the "Here's Lucy" era. Gale Gordon, Lucie Arnaz, Gary Morton, and Richard Burton all appear with Lucy on these odd, and certainly unique, items.

Although she rarely left the sound stage, Lucille Ball could be spotted all over the globe on magazine covers, movie posters, trading cards, and many other articles still waiting to be rediscovered. Today she is no longer with us, but her legacy continues to be a happy part of so many people's lives throughout the world.

Chapter 9

Picturegoer

416

417

Film Weekly 2.d

Lucille BALL

MON COPAIN

LUCILE BALL

Picturegoer

Picturegoer

Lucille BALL

Lucille BALL

419

420

416. *Picturegoer,*
November 29, 1941
(England) (C)

417. *Picturegoer,*
February 17, 1940
(England) (C)

418. *Mon Copain,*
April 25, 1937
(France) (C/D)

419. *Picturegoer,*
March 30, 1946
(England) (C)

420. *Picturegoer,*
April 3, 1943
(England) (C)

418

138 ♥ Lucy in Another Land

421. *Uge-Revyen,*
November 25, 1949
(Denmark) (C)

422.
Uge-Revyen,
November 14,
1950 (Denmark)
(C)

423. *Uge-Revyen,*
February 4, 1947
(Denmark) (C)

424. *Hollywood,*
September 18, 1948
(Italy) (C)

425. *Hollywood,*
November 22, 1947
(Italy) (C)

426. *Cinelandia, July 1947* (Latin America) (C)

427. *Films and Stars of 1948* (Scotland) (C)

428. *Suplemento de Paquita de lunes: Labores e ideas para su hogar, February 6, 1950* (Mexico) (C)

429. *V, October 12, 1947* (France) (C/D)

430. *Negro y blanco labores, May 1947* (Mexico) (C/D)

431. *Paquita de lunes, February 6, 1950* (Mexico) (C/D)

432. *Picture Show*,
June 5, 1954
(England) (C)

433. *Piccolo*,
January 30, 1955
(Belgium) (C/D)

435. *Picture Show*,
September 25, 1943
(England) (C)

436. *Picture Show*,
July 15, 1944
(England) (C)

434. *Ons Land*,
February 5,
1955 (Belgium)
(C/D)

437.
Picture Post,
September 24,
1955 (England)
(C)

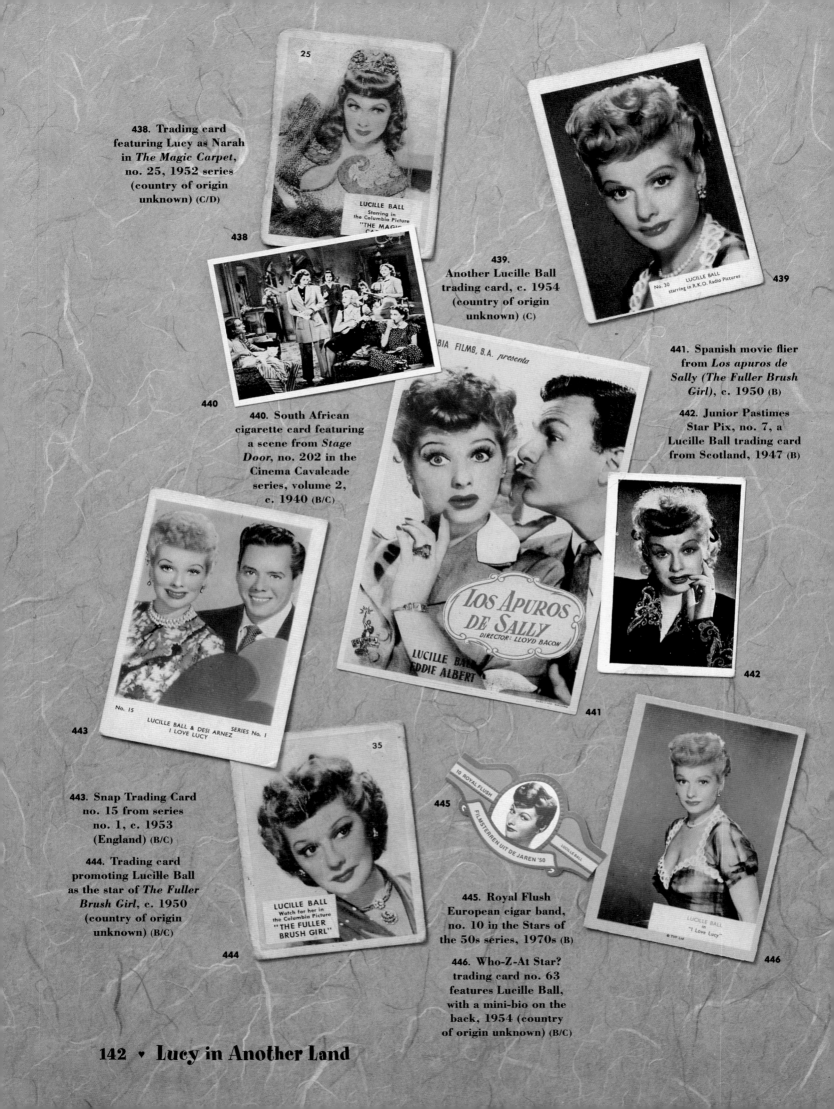

438. Trading card featuring Lucy as Narah in *The Magic Carpet*, no. 25, 1952 series (country of origin unknown) (C/D)

439. Another Lucille Ball trading card, c. 1954 (country of origin unknown) (C)

440. South African cigarette card featuring a scene from *Stage Door*, no. 202 in the Cinema Cavalcade series, volume 2, c. 1940 (B/C)

441. Spanish movie flier from *Los apuros de Sally (The Fuller Brush Girl)*, c. 1950 (B)

442. Junior Pastimes Star Pix, no. 7, a Lucille Ball trading card from Scotland, 1947 (B)

443. Snap Trading Card no. 15 from series no. 1, c. 1953 (England) (B/C)

444. Trading card promoting Lucille Ball as the star of *The Fuller Brush Girl*, c. 1950 (country of origin unknown) (B/C)

445. Royal Flush European cigar band, no. 10 in the Stars of the 50s series, 1970s (B)

446. Who-Z-At Star? trading card no. 63 features Lucille Ball, with a mini-bio on the back, 1954 (country of origin unknown) (B/C)

447. A complete set of 24
Stompkop cigar bands, each
featuring a scene from—or a
star of—"The Lucy Show" or
"Here's Lucy," 1970s
(Belgium) (C)

448. Mexican lobby card from the Bob Hope–Lucille Ball film *Cuando el corazón manda (The Facts of Life)*, 1960s (B/C)

449. Mexican lobby card for *La alfombra magica (The Magic Carpet)*, 1950s (B/C)

450–51. Mexican lobby cards for *Mi pesadilla es un angel (Forever Darling)*, 1950s (each: B/C)

452. Mexican lobby card for *Amor es juego prohibido (The Facts of Life)*, 1960s (B/C)

453. Belgian poster for *Ma Femme est sans critique (Critic's Choice)*, 1960s (B/C)

454. Australian one-sheet movie poster for *Forever Darling*, c. 1956 (B/C)

455. Belgian window card for *Son Ange gardien (Forever Darling)*, 1950s (B/C)

456. British sheet music for "Home Cookin'," 1950 (B)

457. British sheet music for "Havin' A Wonderful Wish (Time You Were Here)," from the film *Sorrowful Jones*, 1949 (B)

458. Canadian *TV Guide*, February 9–15, 1991; compare with the U.S. version (see no. 36, page 23) (A/B)

459. *Star Weekly*, January 25, 1958 (Canada) (B)

460. *Avondlectuur*, July 1971 (Belgium) (C)

461. *Ecran TV*, May 31–June 6, 1966 (Chile) (C)

Get It in Writing

The Lucy Signature

autographed materials, from handwritten letters and autographed photos to signed contracts and revised scripts, are some of the most coveted of all Lucille Ball nostalgia.

When she first went to California in the early 1930s, Lucy had already secured a small part in the Eddie Cantor film *Roman Scandals*. Cast as a slave girl, her only attire was a long blond wig. One of the scarcest of all Lucille Ball autographs stems from this movie. On a vintage 1933 *Roman Scandals* publicity still that pictures her in all her blond glory, she wrote, "Jessie darling, As long as I am in Cal.—you belong to me—Sincerely, Louciel." The early date, the generous amount of handwriting, and, most importantly, the unusual spelling of her name ("Louciel") make this autograph a rare treasure indeed.

Materials featuring the full "Lucille Ball" signature also hold considerable value and generally date from her pretelevision days. Once she became universally known as TV's "Lucy," she usually responded to autograph requests with the more intimate inscription "Love Lucy."

Today Lucille Ball–autographed material occasionally turns up on the collectors' circuit through autograph dealers, Hollywood collectibles shops, and antiques shows. Distinguishing between an authentic autograph and a secretarial signature, however, often requires an expert eye.

Lucy, the Writing Tablet

As unusual as it may seem, throughout the 1960s Lucy could often be spotted heading off to school on the covers of a variety of children's writing tablets. One tablet cover features Lucy with her two children, Lucie and Desi Jr., and TV costar Gale Gordon in a backyard setting. Others display black-and-white glamour shots from her movie days. But probably the most coveted of all Lucy writing tablets is the one featuring a still from the "Lucy and Bob Hope" episode of "I Love Lucy." With Bob Hope "coaching" her, Lucy—"disguised" as a Cleveland Indian—looks like she's just about to catch a ball. The crossover interest from baseball collectors, Cleveland Indians fans, and Bob Hope admirers makes this one highly sought after notebook.

Lucy, the Arcade Card

Throughout the 1940s arcade, or exhibit, cards were a popular vending-machine prize. About the same size as postcards, these heavy-stock cardboard cards featured portraits of virtually every big-name star of the day, including Lucille Ball. As an added attraction, a simulated signature of the celebrity was printed on each card. Today these often-forgotten artifacts of Hollywood's heyday occasionally turn up, to the delight of collectors and fans.

The Lucy Reply

It should come as no surprise that Lucy regularly received fan mail from around the world. Over the years, a variety of photo cards were sent out to well-wishers in response. During the "I Love Lucy" days, black-and-white and color photo cards of Lucy and Desi, featuring facsimiles of their signatures, were mailed out to all the fans who took the time to write to them.

In Lucy's later years, Lucille Ball Productions developed three Lucille Ball fan cards, each a postcard-style contemporary photograph of her, inscribed with a facsimile "Love Lucy" signature.

Personally answering every fan letter was of course impossible. But Lucy appreciated her fans, so when time permitted, she would dip into her mailbag and surprise a few lucky admirers with a personal reply.

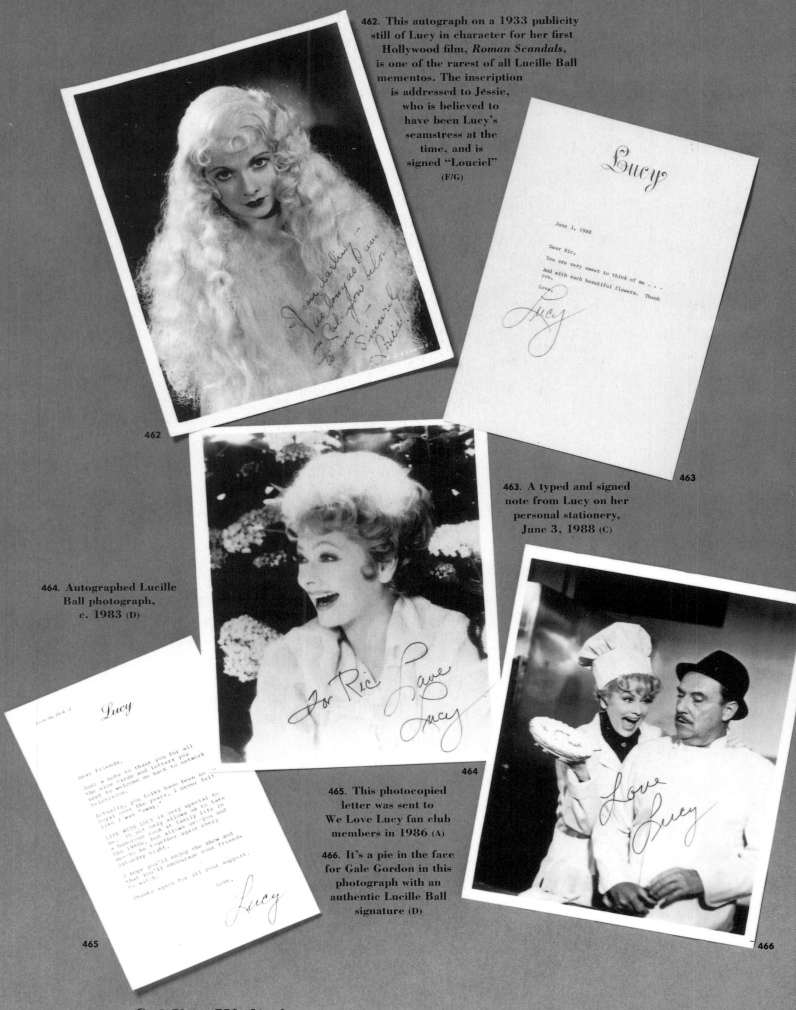

462. This autograph on a 1933 publicity still of Lucy in character for her first Hollywood film, *Roman Scandals*, is one of the rarest of all Lucille Ball mementos. The inscription is addressed to Jessie, who is believed to have been Lucy's seamstress at the time, and is signed "Louciel" (F/G)

463. A typed and signed note from Lucy on her personal stationery, June 3, 1988 (C)

464. Autographed Lucille Ball photograph, c. 1983 (D)

465. This photocopied letter was sent to We Love Lucy fan club members in 1986 (A)

466. It's a pie in the face for Gale Gordon in this photograph with an authentic Lucille Ball signature (D)

467. William Frawley photograph (A)

468. William Frawley's signature (C)

469. Black-and-white autographed photo of Vivian Vance (C)

470. Black-and-white photograph of Vivian Vance and William Frawley as Ethel and Fred Mertz (A)

471. Desi Arnaz leans on his conga drum in this autographed photo, 1983 (C)

472. Little Ricky gets his tie straightened by his TV dad in this photograph with the inscription "Desi" (C)

473. On this black-and-white photograph of a scene from "The Lucy-Desi Comedy Hour" episode "Lucy Goes to Mexico," the inscription reads, "To Ric Wyman From Desi Arnaz" (C/D)

474. This autographed postcard captures Desi Arnaz in the "Homecoming" episode of "I Love Lucy" (B/C)

475. The signature on this publicity photo of Lucy reading *Everywoman*'s magazine is simulated, 1950s (B)

476. This 5 × 7" color publicity photo captures Lucy and Desi during their reign as America's favorite prime-time couple, 1950s (B)

477–79. Heavy-stock Lucille Ball arcade cards, each featuring a simulated signature, 1940s (each: B)

480. A pre-signed publicity photo of Lucy and Desi, 1950s (A)

481. This arcade card dates from the "I Love Lucy" era, 1950s (B)

482, 484. Publicity photos of Lucille Ball the movie star; the signatures are simulated, 1940s (each: A)

483, 485, 488. These fan cards were sent out as replies to admirers who wrote to Lucy, late 1970s (Lucy's poodle, Tinker, poses with her in no. 483) (each: B)

486. Interior of a publicity card, featuring simulated signatures of the stars of "Life With Lucy"; the exterior (not shown) features a full-color Lucille Ball photo on the front and a cast shot on the back, 1986 (B)

487. The autograph on this fan card is also simulated (A)

489

490

10¢

10¢

10¢

0¢

Lucille Ball & Bob Hope

LUCILLE BALL
Metro-Goldwyn-Mayer

Film

29¢ 29¢ 29¢

29¢ 29¢

Desi Arnaz Jr. Gale Gor...

Lucille Ball

A2 SHEETS
7¼ IN x 10 IN

491

492

493

491. Lucy poses as a Cleveland Indian being coached by Bob Hope on the cover of this 10¢ children's notebook (C)

492. Look closely, and you'll see Lucy's name misspelled on this vintage writing tablet, 1940s (C)

494–97. The same image of Lucille Ball appeared on 3 different writing tablets and the wrapper on a package of Movie Stars notebook filler paper, 1940s (each: C)

494

489. One of several rare Lucille Ball writing tablets, 1940s (C)

490. At one time, 29¢ could get any school-bound youngster a Lucy writing tablet; today, collectors pay much more (C)

495

496

493. This tablet features Lucy, Gale Gordon, and Lucy's children, Desi Jr. and Lucie, 1960s (C)

497

"I Love Lucy": "Lucy Is Envious,"
originally broadcast March 29, 1954

The Rare, Unusual, and One-of-a-Kinds

Your Ticket, Please

In the course of Lucille Ball's television career, well over four hundred episodes of her five series were filmed in front of a live studio audience—a concept she and Desi originated. Filming in front of a live audience necessitated the printing and distribution of audience admittance tickets. As audience members entered the studio, the tickets were collected by ushers and later discarded. Today, the few tickets that survive have become rarities. Of course, original tickets from "I Love Lucy" and "The Lucille Ball–Desi Arnaz Show" ("The Lucy-Desi Comedy Hour") hold the greatest value because of their age and the overwhelming popularity of the two series. But tickets from "The Lucy Show," "Here's Lucy," and "Life with Lucy" have also proved to be reasonable investments.

It's in the Script

Each week all of the actors, crew members, hairdressers, and makeup artists participating in the latest episode received a new script. These scripts usually consisted of mimeographed or photocopied pages with heavy-stock colored-paper covers. After completion of an episode, most of the scripts were either returned to the studio or thrown away. Few have survived, making them rare treasures.

Unlike most memorabilia, scripts are often more desirable if they are in worn, marked condition. An old script with handwritten notations not only gives insight into the development of the episode but also holds a unique collectible element if the revisions were written by one of the stars. Imagine the collectibility of a script filled with changes penciled in by Lucy herself!

Lucille's Closet

Costumes, gowns, boas, and other articles from Lucille Ball's personal wardrobe are certainly one-of-a-kind collectibles and quite a few have recently been made available on the auction block. Lucie Arnaz has donated a collection of her mother's personal items to the Chautauqua Arts Council to help raise money for the development of the Lucille Ball–Desi Arnaz Museum in Jamestown, New York (Lucy's hometown). The auction of these items has been a highlight of LucyFest—Jamestown's annual Memorial Day weekend celebration.

The First Lucy Story and Other Uncommon Memorabilia

The story of Lucille Ball's life has been told by many biographers, some less credibly than others. But none is more sought after than the first, *The Real Story of Lucille Ball*, by Eleanor Harris. Published as a paperback in 1953 by Ballantine, and originally priced at 35 cents, this biography recounts the story of "the woman who won the battle of preserving the things she loved—marriage, home, and family—against the unceasing demands of success." Today people are ready and willing, but often not able to locate this rare piece of Lucy memorabilia.

Another uncommon item is the *"I Love Lucy" 3-D Picture Magazine*. Issued in 1953, complete with 3-D viewing glasses, this magazine contains a variety of sepia-toned images taken straight from the television series. They appear blurry to the naked eye, but when viewed through the 3-D glasses, the Ricardos seem to jump right off the pages.

Equally rare is a toy watch bearing images of Lucy and Ricky. It was but one of an entire line of dime-store watches featuring the faces of Hollywood celebrities. Among the subjects depicted on these watches were the Long Ranger, the Three Stooges, Edgar Bergen and Charlie McCarthy, and John Wayne. Consisting of a metal frame, cardboard backing, and a colored elastic band, these nonmechanical toys are quite primitive and contain no copyright markings but are believed to date to the late 1950s.

The Desilu Sales Items

Another unique division of Lucy memorabilia are the items created by the Desilu Sales team in the 1950s and early 1960s. Manufactured in small quantities as gifts for business associates and potential clients, these items include coffee mugs, ashtrays, cigarette lighters, and cufflinks. Each features a caricature of Lucy and/or Desi, and most have the "Desilu Sales Inc." marking. Originally unavailable to the general public, these promotional giveaways are rare finds today.

Lucy's Christmas Presents

Every Christmas, Lucy's friends and business associates would find special presents left under their tree by a redheaded Santa. Glossy black vinyl ice buckets bearing the Lucille Ball Productions logo and a "Love Lucy" inscription were her gifts for one Christmas in the 1970s. Other gifts over the years include drinking glasses, engraved silver trays, and clocks.

In 1986, during the short-lived "Life With Lucy" series, Lucille Ball commissioned special wristwatches displaying both the Lucille Ball Productions logo and a "Love Lucy" inscription on the watch face. Designed in both men's and women's styles, these watches were Lucy's Christmas present to the cast and crew of the show; fewer than a hundred are believed to exist. Each one serves as a timely reminder of Lucy's appreciation for the people who worked for her.

GREEN FLASH
THE CALL BULLETIN

DeMille on Throne Atop Huge Crane Views Monarchy

By HARRISON CARROLL

Copyright 1943, King Features Syndicate Inc.

Today I'll take you to one of the few absolute monarchies left in the world—as Cecil B. de Mille set.

For his picture, "The Story of Dr. Wassell," De Mille has recreated the Javanese port installations at Tjilatjap, just as they were when the battered U. S. cruiser Marblehead disgorged it's wounded before commencing an epic journey almost all the way around the world to a home port.

From his throne atop a camera crane 42 feet in the air, the bald headed De Mille surveys a scene of teeming activity.

In the foreground is a section of the Marblehead, correct even to duplications of Japanese shell holes. In stretchers, the wounded are being carried down the gangplank to the docks. There the stretcher-bearers push their way through a motley throng of Javanese volunteer nurses, other natives and Aussie soldiers. Awaiting them is a hospital train. It's a real train, four antiquated cars hooked to the high stacked engine that Paramount bought for "Union Pacific."

Colorful Character

Among the nurses is Carol Thurston, the 20 year old Montana girl whom De Mille has chosen to play "Three Martini," one of the most colorful feminine characters in the story. She is wearing an authentic Javanese costume—a kemban (similar to the wrap-around brassieres that American girls wear on the beaches) and a true sarong of hand-painted cloth that extends from the waist to the ankles.

Miss Thurston is a diminutive brunette, but equipped with luscious curves, a la Jane Russell. By coincidence, she attended the Billings, Mont. high school, where Gary Cooper, star of the picture, once was a pupil.

The set is out in the open. Occasionally a plane will fly overhead. But, for once, this doesn't interfere with the action.

"People," calls De Mille from his God-like perch, "if a plane flies over during the scenes, don't stop; just look up."

Now, as they are almost ready for the take, a pleasant-faced, gray-haired woman walks onto the set. It is Mrs. De Mille. She squints up at Hollywood's most absolute monarch. A worried look comes over her face.

"Goodness," she murmurs, "he is going to get an awful sunburn on top of his head."

Musical Production

Over at the Goldwyn studios Dinah Shore and Broadway's Danny Kaye are about to do a number for the musical, "Up in Arms." The scene is supposed to be the lobby of the Radio City Music Hall Theater in New York.

There's a long wait for the camera lineup. Both Kaye and Miss Shore are comparative newcomers to the screen. Director Elliott Nugent wants to keep them from tightening up.

"Why don't you go into the 'Zooten Suiten' routine?" he suggests.

The stars need no more encouragement. As they start to sing, the extras gather around in a circle. This is not work, it's fun. And the number is going to be a honey.

After a terrific finish Kaye clowns a bow. "At what other studio," he demands, "do you get such service?"

Roller Skating Scene

First the movies went for ice skaters and now it's roller skaters. Twentieth Century-Fox has hired the "Skating Vanities" troupe to do numbers for "Pin Up Girl."

Director Bruce Humberstone is putting them through their paces on a 50 by 80 masonite rink. Star of the troupe is 20 year old Gloria Nordskog, a Norwegian like Sonja Henie, whom she idolizes. She started skating at 15 and Sid Grauman, old-time impresario of the Grauman's Chinese Theater, first encouraged her to be a professional.

Miss Nordskog is a dainty blond with a dazzling smile. Her legs are slender but strong. They have to be strong because her professional skates, with the shoes, weigh eight pounds.

The "Skating Vanities" is a new outfit, with only one tour under its belt, but according to Manager Harold Steinman, it's going places.

"How can we fail?" he asks. "We are giving them a production like a 'Ziegfeld Follies.' And look at the field we have. There are only 250 ice rinks in this country, but there are 4,500 roller skating rinks. After this picture we really ought to be hot!"

A few lengths of fabric and a scattering of starry sequins make a fetching "costume" for Lucille Ball, who is both cute and comical in "DuBarry Was a Lady," now playing at the Fox Theater.

Mendocino Coa[st] England for [

Paramount Cast Work[s] Albion in Du Maurier [

By FRED JOHNSON

It was still California's Mendocino [coast] reminded on a northward drive along th[e] highway. It had long been just that to [us] through the Redwood Empire.

But soon, as the blue Pacific looms, it [is] coast of England. And Paramount stu[dio] filmers of Daphne Du Maurier's "French[man's Creek"] have known it as nothing else for the las[t]

It was more or less coincidence that [this] Technicolor film had moved into a ghost [town] named Albion by its first settlers as a fur[ther reminder of] their native Britain. It was less coincide[nce that the] studio had picked this bit of shoreline [as an] exact duplicate of the Cornish coast, [with] bracken on the moors atop its cliffs an[d] berry brambles along its roadways.

Our Locations Popular

This location choice was in the cou[rse of Holly]wood's gradual discovery of northern [California as a] movie wonderland, after similar discov[eries] around Santa Cruz, Sonora, Chico, San[ta Rosa,] Healdsburg.

One thing the movie people didn't kno[w—]the existence near old Albion of a Frenc[h] so named by its settlers long before Mis[s Du Maurier] began dreaming up her novel. It seems th[at it was] some Frenchmen who had been shipwre[cked near the] little stream.

We can forget the British who had [followed] Drake into his bay further down the c[oast, the] Russians who had settled near by at F[ort Ross] in another stronghold above Fort Bragg[, and those who] are in Cornwall. And those remaining s[ome] of the 400 households that once had clun[g to the] sides above Albion Creek were free to go [about] fishing and farming apart from this En[glish town of the] seventeenth century. But they'd rather [be in the] strange business of making a movie.

Navigation Problems

They wonder at the presence in their [bay of] an ancient pirate ship, rebuilt from that [of Cecil] B. DeMille's in "Reap the Wild Wind," [and] towed the 600 miles from San Pedro a[nd up a] channel dredged to let it in. There was [trouble] getting it past the highway bridge.

In the dredging process a million [feet of] sunken logs were salvaged from the stre[am to be used] for rebuilding of old houses on the hillsi[de] for some 200 members of the location t[roupe—a] bit of Paramount wartime economy as it [is spend]ing $16,000 a day in the making of ["Frenchman's] Creek."

Actors are housed in cottages and aut[o camps along] the highway or in picturesque Little Rive[r, where] colorful Director Mitchell Leisen has ins[talled his own] cook and butler. A boarding and supply [house is] made of Albion a new type of boomtown fo[r the $2,000,-] 000 picture, guided by Leisen following h[is success] of "Lady in the Dark" at a cost of one-th[ird as much.]

No Wolf at Door Here

Should Leisen's cook desert and his p[ersonal] line be cut, his entourage at the inn could[n't starve] for a time. "Mitch's" own cookery is ai[ded by] the hotel vegetable garden, in which he to[ps off his] activity's sake when foy interrupts his sh[ooting sched]ule, is bountiful in luscious foods and th[e river pro]vides a salmon fit for the gods. Choices [from the] day's catch he tenderly nurses from oven [to table for] his weekend guests, midway of a heavenl[y ride, or a] special concocting and an Albion bis[que of] creamed extra thick. When food rationin[g is] recalled, as it is not for one lip-smacking [moment, he] might belong in another and distant s[phere—but not] with everything Hollywood.

Sunshine—to Order?

An actor's director is this fun-loving [man, trou]bled by little except the timid aim that [fills] Mendocino's vapors for days on end, afte[r a welcome] stretch of sunny days that had made ever[yone happy.] If fog were wanted, there were smokepot[s aplenty.] So the story goes that a lady of old Albio[n, impressed] by the magic of Hollywood, soberly inqui[red if] light couldn't be as easily invoked—witho[ut] the aid of a modern Gideon.

While sunlight is a necessity, Leisen is [providing] certain film luxuries, such as the rare [18th] century rooms he has bought for the Cor[nish castle of] Navron, home of the Dona St. Colomb, w[ho runs off] with a pirate. The castle has been pa[inted] on a hillside in accord with Leisen's perso[nal plan,] and you can wager the stage coach that [rolls up to] it in one scene is just as authentic.

Fun has its place on a film location a[s a daily] chore, but at his job this former art dire[ctor has] the skill and authority expected of a dire[ctor who is] to some of Hollywood's most expensive pr[oducts.]

Imposing Cast There

Not inexpensive or low bracketed, eithe[r, is the cast] —Joan Fontaine, as Dona St. Colomb; F[rank] her husband; Mexican Arturo De Cordov[a, the pirate] she falls for; Basil Rathbone, the "other [man";] Bruce, Cecil Kellaway, Doris Lloyd and M[any others,] to name a few. Aldo Nadi, a world cham[pion fencer,] is on hand to coach De Cordova and Da[rk, the up-and-] coming young actor and protege of Leise[n.]

The richly gowned Lady Dona is one [she plays] before the cameras. At other times she is q[uite another] —the pigtailed, plainly frocked girl of the [cottage vin]tage, but with a cook and maid in attenda[nce—as] you already know, is Joan Fontaine.

Actor Brian Aherne, with whom we [visited] Albion, identifies her for us almost inst[antly—] still in pigtails and the cotton frock, she t[alks to a] town hermit and negotiates the square [boss] lumbermen of the Paul Bunyan clan at a [friendly] farewell party in her honor. No sign of [the poise dis]posed by this Academy award winner as [she is seen] scaling cliffs and battling on the side of D[e Cor]dova and his grimy crew.

At the dance microphone Aherne—no[w an in]structor at the R. A. F. base in Phoenix—[an]nounces he's mad at Leisen, at almost eve[ry turn, for] he hadn't seen his wife for weeks until r[ecently when] she isn't coming home. He hopes there'l[l be no] more gobs of fog.

(There is—and in a few days all but [the] second unit packs up and goes home.)

499. Picture-frame manufacturers of the 1940s and 1950s often inserted images of movie stars such as Lucille Ball into the frames to entice consumers (C)

500. These primitive five-and-dime-store toy watches didn't tell time, but they did feature miniature photos of Hollywood entertainers, including Edgar Bergen and Charlie McCarthy, the Lone Ranger, the Three Stooges, and Lucy and Desi (C)

498. The Saturday, July 24, 1943, issue of the *San Francisco Call Bulletin* features a dazzling photograph of Lucille Ball, star of *Du Barry Was a Lady*, on its "Green Flash" page (C)

501. One of the rare artifacts from Desilu Sales Inc. is this coffee mug with a caricature of Lucy, 1950s (D/E)

502. This promotional *Mame* ashtray features a "Love Lucy" inscription, 1974 (C)

504. This wristwatch, featuring the Lucille Ball Productions logo and "Love Lucy" signature was created in 1986 as Lucy's Christmas gift for the cast and crew of "Life With Lucy" (E)

503. Like the coffee mug (no. 501), this Desilu Sales ashtray was a promotional item intended to be given to Desilu employees and clients; ashtrays and mugs with a caricature of Desi were also produced (D)

Rare, Unusual, and One-of-a-Kinds ♥ 157

505. This studio audience ticket admits one to the February 17, 1950, broadcast of "My Favorite Husband," Lucy's CBS Radio comedy program (E)

506. The studio audience ticket for the filming of the "Lucy and John Wayne" episode of "I Love Lucy," September 15, 1955, is exceptionally rare (F)

509. Invitation to "Lucy Takes a Cruise to Havana," the first episode of "The Lucille Ball–Desi Arnaz Show," June 28, 1957 (E/F)

508. "Special TV film preview" ticket to the "Lucy Wins a Racehorse" episode of "The Lucille Ball–Desi Arnaz Show," with special guest stars Betty Grable and Harry James, January 16, 1958 (E/F)

510. Ticket to a preview of the "Lucy Goes to Alaska" episode of "The Lucille Ball–Desi Arnaz Show," January 26, 1959 (E/F)

511. Ticket to a preview of "The Ricardos Go to Japan," another episode of "The Lucille Ball–Desi Arnaz Show," November 11, 1959 (E/F)

512. As this vintage ticket attests, on September 30, 1956, Lucy and Desi were guests on "The Ed Sullivan Show" (D/E)

513. The Beverly Hilton Hotel played host to the Friars Club of California Life Achievement Award Dinner honoring Lucille Ball on November 4, 1977 (C/D)

507. Invitation to the "Lucy Hunts Uranium" episode of "The Lucille Ball–Desi Arnaz Show," with special guest stars Fred MacMurray and June Haver, November 15, 1957 (E/F)

514. Loose pages from the script for "Lucy Buys a Boat," a 1963 episode of "The Lucy Show" (N/A)

515. Script for the "Lucy Is a Bird-Sitter" episode of "Here's Lucy," August 16, 1973 (note: the name of Lucy's hairdresser, Irma Kusely, is written on the cover) (C)

516. Studio audience ticket for the "Here's Lucy" episode filmed on July 17, 1969 (D)

517. Studio audience ticket for the "Here's Lucy" episode filmed on October 1, 1970 (D)

518. Studio audience ticket for "Lucy and the Guard Goose," an untelevised episode of "Life With Lucy," July 24, 1986 (C)

519. Studio audience ticket to "One Good Grandparent Deserves Another," the first episode of "Life With Lucy," July 18, 1986 (C)

FIRST DRAFT
June 25, 1986

"Life With Lucy"

Episode #L-002
"Lucy and the Guard Goose"

521. Script for the
"Lucy and the Runaway
Butterfly" episode of
"The Lucy Show,"
March 18, 1963 (C)

520. First-draft script
of the "Lucy and the
Guard Goose" episode
of "Life With Lucy,"
June 25, 1986 (B)

522. First-draft script for
the "Lucy Makes Curtis
Byte the Dust" episode of
"Life With Lucy," dated
September 4, 1986 (B)

THE LUCY SHOW

"LUCY AND THE RUNAWAY BUTTERFLY"
(formerly "LUCY AND THE RUNAWAY...

FIRST DRAFT

September 4, 1986

Mr 26 63

THE LUCY SHOW

"LUCY BUYS A BOAT"

"Life With Lucy"

Episode #L-008
"Lucy Makes Curtis Byte The Dust"

Written by

Arthur Marx

and

Robert Fisher

The Spelling/Ball Joint Venture
© 1986 All Rights Reserved

A LUCILLE BALL PRODUCTION
in association with
AARON SPELLING PRODUCTIONS
1041 North Formosa Avenue
West Hollywood, California 90046

Property of DESILU PRODUCTIONS, INC.

523. Script for the "Lucy
Buys a Boat" episode
of "The Lucy Show,"
March 26, 1963 (C)

160 ♥ Rare, Unusual, and One-of-a-Kinds

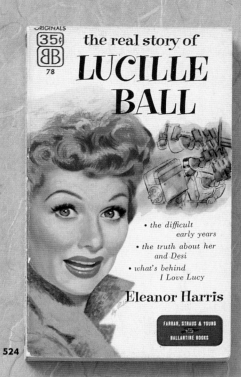

524. Eleanor Harris's *The Real Story of Lucille Ball* is the first and rarest biography of Lucille Ball, 1954 (C)

525. Children once beat out their own rendition of "Babalu" on this hard-to-find toy Desi Arnaz conga drum, 1950s (F/G)

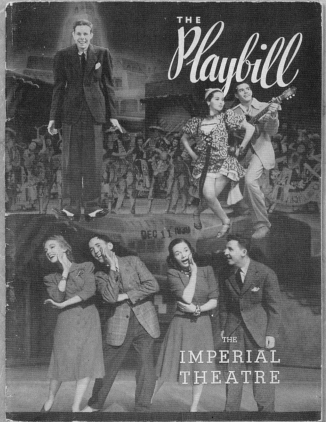

526. This *I Love Lucy* 3-D magazine is a favorite among collectors and fans, 1953 (D)

527. As the cover of this *Playbill* indicates, the Broadway musical *Too Many Girls* featured a young Desi Arnaz, 1939 (C)

528. This aqua ostrich-feather vest must have been one of Lucy's favorite garments (F/G)

528

529. *TV Star Parade* spotted Lucy wearing the vest on an outing with Gary Morton and Desi Arnaz Jr., 1968

529

162 ♥ Rare, Unusual, and One-of-a-Kinds

530–31. Lucy was captured wearing the vest on the covers of two magazines

530. *TV Radio Mirror,*
June 1971 (see also
no. 363) (A/B)

531. *TV Star Parade,*
June 1968 (see also
no. 357) (A/B)

**"The Lucy Show": "Lucy and Carol Burnett, Part 2,"
originally broadcast December 11, 1967**

The Lucy Revival

Lucille Ball's enduring popularity, combined with the nostalgia craze of recent years, has generated the production of a wide variety of Lucy-related items, ranging from greeting cards and collector's plates to key chains and dolls. Some say this Lucy Revival began back in 1978, when Radiola Records preserved a sampling of Lucy's early work on the *I Love Lucy/My Favorite Husband* album. One side acquaints listeners with an episode of Lucille Ball's late 1940s radio show, "My Favorite Husband"; the other offers the audio track from a 1953 "I Love Lucy" episode, "Breaking the Lease." Then, in 1981 Star Merchants released the record *Musical Moments from "I Love Lucy,"* reviving some of Ricky Ricardo's most unforgettable performances. That same year the *"I Love Lucy" Quiz Book* by Bart Andrews was published. It contains more than a thousand questions about the stars and plots of the classic situation comedy. The following year artist Mike Hagel designed a brightly colored collector's plate in honor of the First Lady of Comedy. Featuring four different images of Lucille Ball on a dark yellow background, this limited-edition plate measures just over ten inches in diameter. Each hand-numbered plate is made of Royal Manor porcelain and bordered with twenty-four-karat gold.

A year later, the American Postcard company released a series of sepia-toned postcards featuring classic "I Love Lucy" scenes. Color postcards capturing moments from "The Lucy-Desi Comedy Hour" soon followed.

In 1985 Columbia House Video began issuing episodes of "I Love Lucy" on videocassette. At first these cassettes could be purchased only by mail, but today well-stocked video stores are sure to carry them for rental or sale.

Another 1985 Lucy collectible was a doll produced by the Effanbee Doll Company for its Limited-Edition Legend Series. The inspiration for the doll was the Lucy marionette seen tap-dancing in top hat and tails during the opening credits of the "Here's Lucy" show. In 1988 the four stars of "I Love Lucy" were turned into nineteen-inch vinyl dolls by Presents, a division of Hamilton Gifts.

Since 1977, the members of We Love Lucy: The International Lucille Ball Fan Club have been celebrating their favorite star through a quarterly newsletter developed by the organization's president, Tom Watson. Originally called *Star Notes,* the newsletter was renamed *Celebrating Lucy* for a time and then in 1983 was retitled *Lucy.* On its pages, *Lucy* informed readers of Lucille Ball's current projects and reminisced about Desilu programs of the past. In 1987 a "Let's Ask Lucy" column was introduced, giving members the opportunity to address questions to the lady herself.

Shortly thereafter the newsletter took a five-year hiatus. During this time Lucille Ball died, so when publication resumed in 1992, the newsletter's focus changed to keeping her memory alive. It readopted its original name, *Star Notes,* and ever since, from its new headquarters in Sherman Oaks, California, it has served as a literary meeting place for Lucille Ball admirers. In every issue subscribers not only learn fascinating facts about Lucy's life and career but also share stories of their collecting experiences and find out about new collectibles on the market.

In the years since her death on April 26, 1989, more and more nostalgia items have been developed, including "I Love Lucy" greeting cards, wall calendars, buttons, and board games. In 1989 the Hamilton Collection issued the first in a series of "I Love Lucy" collector's plates. Nine different plates have been produced; eight re-create a classic Lucy moment, and one features a collage of memorable scenes. The Hamilton Collection also created four porcelain "I Love Lucy" dolls: Lucy Ricardo; Ricky Ricardo; Lucy as the Queen of the Gypsies; and Lucy as the Vitameatavegamin girl.

Since 1991, when Universal Studios in Hollywood opened Lucy: A Tribute, a Lucille Ball museum authorized by Lucie Arnaz, a multitude of Lucy souvenirs have been available at Universal's gift shops, including wall clocks, note pads, drinking glasses, suspenders, ashtrays, and blankets. The museum's great popularity prompted Universal to open a second museum at its Florida theme park.

Other products that have contributed to the Lucy revival are "I Love Lucy" neckties (Ralph Marlin Company), two glamorously attired porcelain Lucille Ball dolls (Hollywood Walk of Fame Collection), *I Love Lucy Too* comic books (Eternity Comics), and The *"I Love Lucy" Cookbook* (Abbeville Press).

The Emmy-award-winning documentary "Lucy and Desi: A Home Movie," directed by Lucie Arnaz, is now available on videocassette, as are episodes of "The Lucy-Desi Comedy Hour" and many vintage Lucille Ball films. "I Love Lucy" trading cards have become popular with fans both young and old, and each year LucyFest in Lucille Ball's hometown of Jamestown, New York, generates new pieces of Lucy memorabilia.

Thanks to the constant broadcasting of Lucy's TV series and films on cable networks and local channels across the country, a whole new generation is growing up loving Lucy. Nick-at-Nite, the Nickelodeon cable network's evening and late-night programming, has brought back three of her classic series: "I Love

532

533

Lucy," "The Lucy Show," and "The Lucy-Desi Comedy Hour." The channel hails Lucille Ball as TV's "greatest comic actress of all time." The American Movie Classics cable network frequently presents early Lucille Ball films, and local channels everywhere hold annual Lucy marathons on August 6, her birthday.

The Jackson and Perkins rose company has honored Lucy with the creation of a hybrid tea rose that bears her name. Its blooms, of course, are the color

534

of her hair. And it's only a matter of time before the U.S. Postal Service issues a commemorative Lucille Ball stamp.

The Lucy Revival shows no signs of abating. In so many ways— on television, in the blooming of a rose, and in an overwhelming array of memorabilia— Lucille Ball lives on. The key to her timeless appeal lies in her incomparable ability to make us laugh, and every piece of memorabilia captures a little bit of that extraordinary gift.

535

536

537

538

532. "California, Here We Come," first in a series of eight "I Love Lucy" collector's plates by Jim Kritz from the Hamilton Collection, 1989 (D)

533. "A Night at the Copa," seventh in the Hamilton Collection series, 1991 (C)

534. "The Lucille Ball Tribute Plate" by artist Mike Hagel, the first Lucille Ball collector's plate, 1982 (D/E)

539

535. "A Rising Problem," eighth in the Hamilton Collection series, 1991 (C)

536. "Eating the Evidence," fourth in the Hamilton Collection series, 1990 (C)

537. "Two of a Kind," fifth in the Hamilton Collection series, 1990 (C)

538. "The Big Squeeze," third in the Hamilton Collection series, 1989 (C)

540

539. "Lucy" by Morgan Weistling, Hamilton Collection, 1992 (C)

540. "Queen of the Gypsies," sixth in the Hamilton Collection series, 1990 (C)

541. "Just Like Candy," second in the Hamilton Collection series, 1989 (C)

541

543

544

545

542. The Hamilton Collection's Vitameatavegamin doll comes complete with spoon and bottle in hand, 1992 (D)

543. Hamilton's Queen of the Gypsies doll is modeled after Lucy Ricardo's role as Camille in the "Operetta" episode of "I Love Lucy," 1991 (D)

544. Hamilton's Ricky Ricardo doll was an instant sellout, 1990; originally priced at $99.50, it now brings $400 or more (E)

545. Hamilton's first porcelain Lucille Ball doll, Lucy Ricardo, 1990 (D/E)

542

546

547

546–47. While the Hamilton Collection caught Lucille Ball's classic "I Love Lucy" look, artist Corliss Scott captured her more glamorous side in two limited-edition dolls for the Hollywood Walk of Fame Collection.

546. Lucille Ball in Blue, 1993 (D/E)

547. 1989 Academy Awards Lucille Ball, 1993 (D/E)

548

548. In 1985, the Effanbee Doll Company chose Lucille Ball as the subject of their Limited-Edition Legend Series; originally priced at $85, today this doll sells for considerably more, 1985 (D)

549–52: "I Love Lucy" vinyl collector's dolls by
Presents, a division of Hamilton Gifts.

549. Fred Mertz, 1988 (C)   **551. Ricky Ricardo,** 1988 (C)
550. Ethel Mertz, 1988 (C)   **552. Lucy Ricardo,** 1988 (C)

553. Radiola Records released the *I Love Lucy/My Favorite Husband* album in 1978 (B)

I Love Lucy

Exactly as heard on the CBS Radio network, February 27, 1951; sponsored by Philip Morris. With Lucille Ball, Desi Arnaz, Vivian Vance, William Frawley; John Stevenson announcing.

Lucille Ball Desi Arnaz

553

555. The *Musical Moments from "I Love Lucy"* record album was released by Star Merchants in 1981 (A)

554. This unique holiday CD was produced to promote the CBS/FOX Home Video release "A TV Christmas Present." Issued in a limited edition of 2,000, it was distributed to radio stations during the 1990 Christmas season and was not available to the general public (B/C)

554

MUSICAL MOMENTS FROM

I Love Lucy

Celebrating the 30th Anniversary

555

556. *The Long, Long Trailer,* Lucy and Desi's most memorable film together, is now available on videocassette, 1990 (A)

557. The Columbia House Video Library has preserved all thirteen episodes of "The Lucy-Desi Comedy Hour" on videotape, 1993 (each: A)

558. The secrets, silliness, and blunders not included in "Lucy And Desi: A Home Movie" can be seen on *The Outtakes,* a videocassette distributed by Arluck Entertainment, 1993 (A)

559. Lucie Arnaz and Desi Arnaz Jr. talk candidly about their parents on a thirty-minute video, *Lucie & Desi Jr.: The Interview,* Arluck Entertainment, 1993 (A)

563. Today, video stores and retail chains everywhere carry CBS/Fox "I Love Lucy" videotapes, each featuring three episodes from the classic show, 1989 (each: A)

560. Lucille Ball and Henry Fonda star in the 1968 MGM comedy *Yours, Mine and Ours,* now available on videotape, 1989 (A)

561. The videotape version of the Emmy-award-winning documentary "Lucy and Desi: A Home Movie" contains footage not seen on television, Arluck Entertainment, 1993 (A)

562. The once-lost "I Love Lucy" pilot has been packaged on videocassette as "*I Love Lucy*": *The Very First Show,* 1994 (A)

The Lucy Revival ♥ 173

567–72. Landmark's "I Love Lucy" wall calendars capture a year's worth of timeless moments from one of America's best-loved situation comedies

567. 1995 "I Love Lucy" calendar (A)
568. 1993 "I Love Lucy" calendar (A)
569. 1991 "I Love Lucy" calendar (A)
570. 1990 "I Love Lucy" calendar (A)
571. 1994 "I Love Lucy" calendar (A)
572. 1992 "I Love Lucy" calendar (A)

564. *The "I Love Lucy" Cookbook*, Abbeville Press, 1994 (A)

565. Now out of print, Bart Andrews's *The "I Love Lucy" Quiz Book* is on the top of many fans' "want lists," A.S. Barnes & Company, 1981 (B/C)

566. Relive your favorite episodes while playing the "I Love Lucy" board game, Talicor, 1990 (A)

568

567

570

569

571

572

573

574

573

FUNNY IN FF

FRED'S MASTERPIECE

HANDY DANDY LUCY

THEY CALL HER SALLY SWEET

FOILED AGAIN

BOSOM B

SEEING DOUBLE

HILLBILLY HEAVEN

I LOVE LUCY "JOB SWITCHING" with Elvia Allman as the Supervisor
Episode #39 Originally Broadcast September 15, 1952

I Love Lucy

573. In 1991 Pacific Trading Cards produced 110 different "I Love Lucy" trading cards (A)

574. American Postcards began printing a wide variety of "I Love Lucy" postcards in 1983. The licensing agreement was recently picked up by Classico, a San Francisco–based postcard company (A)

574

575. *Lucy: We Love You* tribute magazine, 1989 (B)

577

Lucille Ball

578

579

579. *Lucy: A Loving Tribute*, tribute magazine, 1989 (B)

576

576. *Lucy: We Love You* tribute magazine, 1990 (B)

577. **Lucille Ball: Hollywood Walk of Fame Star postcard, 1980s (A)**

578. **Desi Arnaz: Hollywood Walk of Fame Star postcard, 1980s (A)**

580

580. *Lucy: A Loving Tribute*, tribute magazine, 1990 (B)

COLOMBIANOS Y PERICO 'MUERDEN' P. 48

ALEMANIA ASUSTA A HOLANDA POR EL MUNDIAL '90 P. 42

el diario /la prensa

ADIOS LUCY

Dejó un millón de carcajadas para cada uno de nosotros

LOTTO DE PENN

NEW YORK POST

THURSDAY, APRIL 27, 1989 / SPORTS FINAL

WE LOVED LUCY

TV, screen legend dead at age

582

Abortion issue's day in to...

DAILY NEWS

2 PARK TEENS ARE INDICTED

Victim takes turn for worse

WE LOVED LUCY

584

LUCY DIES

SEE TODAY'S

NEW YORK POST

583

OLD ST. PATRICK'S CHURCH

LUCILLE BALL

(1911 - 1989)

MEMORIAL MASS
MONDAY, MAY 8, 1989
700 WEST ADAMS
CHICAGO, ILLINOIS

585

LUCILLE BALL MORTON
August 6, 1911 – April 26, 1989

Our family was so deeply moved by your thoughtful expression of sympathy...

And we are lucky, indeed, to have had so much love and support from those who we know loved her as much as we did.

Love,
The Ball-Arnaz-Morton family

586

581. *El Diario,*
April 27, 1989 (A)

582. *New York Post,*
April 27, 1989 (A)

581

584. *New York Daily
News,* April 27, 1989 (A)

583. *New York Post
"Lucy Dies"
poster, April 27,
1989* (A)

585. Program from
the Lucille Ball
memorial service at
Old St. Patrick's
Church, Chicago,
May 8, 1989 (B)

586. The Ball-Arnaz-
Morton family sent this
memorial photograph
with thank-you note on
the reverse to the
thousands of admirers
who sent condolences
after Lucy's death (B)

The Lucy Revival ♥ 179

588

593

594

587. *Lucy,* vol. 2, no. 1, Autumn 1983 (A)
588. *Lucy,* vol. 2, no. 2, Spring 1984 (A)

590

591

587

592. *Lucy,* Winter 1985 (A)
593. *Lucy,* special issue no. 4, 1987 (A)
594. *Lucy,* Spring 1986 (A)
595. *Lucy,* Fall 1985 (A)

600

589. *Lucy,* vol. 2, no. 3, Summer 1984 (A)
590. *Lucy,* vol. 2, no. 4, Autumn 1984 (A)
591. *Lucy,* vol. 2, no. 5, Winter/Spring, 1985 (A)

589

587–607. The quarterly magazine of We Love Lucy: The International Lucille Ball Fan Club has changed its name over the years but not its devotion to its subject. For information, write We Love Lucy, P.O. Box 56234, Sherman Oaks, CA 91413

598

597

596

599

602. *Star Notes,*
Autumn 1992 (A)
603. *Star Notes,*
Spring 1993 (A)

608. "We Love Lucy"
button, 1992 (A)

609. We Love Lucy:
The International
Lucille Ball Fan Club
membership cards,
1980s (each A)

596. *Celebrating Lucy,*
April 1981 (A)

597. *Celebrating Lucy,*
June–July 1981 (A)

598. *Celebrating Lucy,*
August–September
1981 (A)

599. *Celebrating Lucy,*
August–October
1982 (A)

600. *Celebrating*
Lucy, April–May
1982 (A)

601. *Celebrating Lucy,*
June–July 1982 (A)

604. *Star Notes,*
Indian Summer 1993 (A)
605. *Star Notes,*
Winter 1993 (A)

606. *Star Notes, no. 5,*
Spring 1994 (A)
607. *Star Notes, no. 6,*
Summer 1994 (A)

610–23: Eternity's *I Love Lucy* and *I Love Lucy Too!* comic books provide a nostalgic look at one of television's most beloved sitcoms

610. *I Love Lucy* comic book, no. 1, June 1990 (A/B)

613. *I Love Lucy in Full Color* comic book, no. 1, 1991 (A/B)

612. *I Love Lucy* comic book, no. 2, June 1990 (A/B)

615. *I Love Lucy* comic book, no. 3, July 1990 (A/B)

611. *I Love Lucy* comic book, no. 4, August 1990 (A/B)

616. *I Love Lucy* comic book, no. 5, September 1990 (A/B)

614. *I Love Lucy* comic book, no. 6, October 1990 (A/B)

619. *I Love Lucy Too!* comic book, no. 2, November 1990 (A)

619

617

617. *I Love Lucy Too!* comic book, no. 1, November 1990 (A)

620

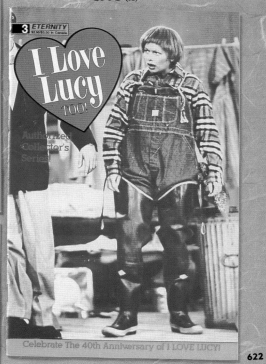

620. *I Love Lucy Too!* comic book, no. 5, February 1991 (A)

621. *I Love Lucy in 3-D!* comic book, no 1, 1991 (A)

622

622. *I Love Lucy Too!* comic book, no. 3, December 1990 (A)

618

618. *I Love Lucy Too!* comic book, no. 4, January 1991 (A)

621

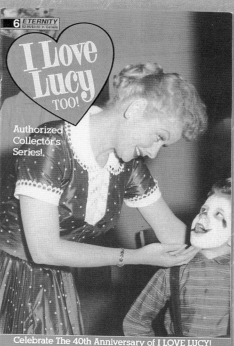

623

623. *I Love Lucy Too!* comic book, no. 6, March 1991 (A)

625

627

628

629

626

631

LAURENCE LUCKINBILL
as CLARENCE DARROW
May 22, 1992

Lucille Ball

632

634

Lucy
A TRIBUTE
UNIVERSAL STUDIOS

635

Lucy : A TRIBUTE
OPENING CELEBRATION
Saturday, April 13, 1991

UNIVERSAL STUDIOS

VIP TRAM TO STUDIO CENTER
DEPARTS FROM SHERATON-UNIVERSAL HOTEL
BALLROOM ENTRANCE

8:00 PM   HORS D'OEUVRES, DANCING & ENTERTAINMENT
"TROPICANA CLUB"
UNIVERSAL STUDIOS HOLLYWOOD-STUDIO CENTER

Till
11:00 PM   Dress Warmly
Present this ticket at the Lucy Tribute to receive your complimentary photo

April 13, 1991   Universal Studios Hollywood

№ 103

636

Lucy
A TRIBUTE

633

630

Lucille Ball
'LITTLE THEATRE
OF JAMESTOWN'

We ♥ Lu
1st Anniv

639

AUCTION
from the Estate of Lucille Ball
SATURDAY, MAY 28, 1994
SALE BEGINS AT 7:00 P.M.
Preview 3:00-7:00 P.M.
Admission $3.00
Catalog $5.00

LOCATION:
THE REG LENNA
CIVIC CENTER
16 East Third St.
Jamestown, NY 14701
(716) 484-7070

Holiday Inn, (716) 664-3400

Auctioneers for

638

Lucille Ball
FESTIVAL
OF NEW COMEDY
STATION
JAMESTOWN, NY 14701 • MAY 23, 1991

637

635. **Ticket to the
opening of the Lucy:
A Tribute museum,
April 13, 1991** (B)

636. **Invitation to the
opening of the Lucy:
A Tribute museum,
1991** (B)

637. **Commemorative
"first-day" stamp
cancellations,
Jamestown, New York,
1989, 1990, and 1991**
(each: A)

646. **"I Love Lucy" greeting cards,
Ambassador, 1990** (each: A)

640

Lucille Ball
FESTIVAL
OF NEW COMEDY

Loves
friendly people... friendly prices

Lucy
LOVES
LUCY FEST

17 - 24, 1992
the Post-Journal

641

JAMESTOWN, NY
716·484·7070
Info & Tickets
Don't miss the excitement
...ort the Festival, Call

642

ORCHESTRA
CTR   A   23
$35.00
The Last Laugh
The Gala Finale
Sunday, May 24, 1992
Vaudeville Finale & Gala Reception

Lucille Ball
Festival
of New
Comedy
Tour

HOLLYWOOD

643

RED ARNAZ

644

I Love Lucy
Lucille Ball
I STILL LOVE LUCY

645

I Love Lucy
MEMBER
FAN ♥ CLUB
The above member is sworn to uphold the high standards of
trusted family entertainment that this television show has
enjoyed for over thirty years
ED MAFFEI, President

643. **One of a series of Hollywood
Walk of Fame trading cards, Starline,
Inc., 1991** (A)

644. **Lucille Ball pin-back buttons,
1980s** (each: A)

645. **"I Love Lucy" fan club
membership card, early 1980s** (A)

642. **Lucille Ball Festival of New Comedy closing
night gala ticket stub, May 24, 1992** (A)

185

Starring Lucille Ball

As a child, Lucille Ball often spent her Saturdays attending the local vaudeville shows in Jamestown, New York, with her Grandpa Hunt. The antics she saw on stage captivated her, and she knew even then what she wanted to do with her life. So in her teens Lucille left Jamestown and headed off to New York City, where her mother enrolled her in the John Murray Anderson–Robert Milton School of Theater and Dance. But within six weeks she was back home. She had been told she had no talent.

Determined to prove herself nonetheless, Lucille later returned to New York. Living in inexpensive hotels and boarding houses, she worked as a clerk in a drugstore and landed a job as a model for dress designer Hattie Carnegie. In 1933 her modeling experience won her a spot as a Chesterfield cigarette girl. Later that year, while walking down a New York City street on a sweltering July day, Lucille bumped into an agent she knew. The agent mentioned that she needed one more showgirl for a film project in Hollywood. There was no time for a screen test, and Lucille got the job.

Four days later, she was on her way to California for one of the longest apprenticeships in Hollywood history, appearing in more than fifteen films before seeing her name in the credits. She worked at Columbia, RKO, and then MGM, where she was filmed in color as a redhead for the first time. Eventually dubbed Queen of the B's, Lucille Ball was not destined to achieve true stardom in her film career.

But in 1948, with some sixty-five movies and numerous guest appearances on radio to her credit, Lucille Ball landed a starring role in "My Favorite Husband," a weekly CBS Radio comedy program that presented the day-to-day life of a banker and his wonderfully zany wife. The series was a great success and ran for three years.

In 1951 Lucy and her real-life husband, Cuban singer Desi Arnaz, decided to tackle a new entertainment medium known as television. Their half-hour comedy program for CBS, "I Love Lucy," premiered on October 15 and became a fixture on Monday nights for the next six years. It brought Lucille Ball the stardom that had eluded her on the big screen and remains the most popular situation comedy in television history.

"The Lucy-Desi Comedy Hour" succeeded "I Love Lucy" in 1957 and continued until Lucille Ball and Desi Arnaz divorced in 1960. Each of the show's hour-long episodes featured big-name guest stars, including Tallulah Bankhead, Fred MacMurray, Danny Thomas, and Milton Berle. Lucy then took a hiatus from television to star on Broadway in *Wildcat*. But she returned to television in October 1962 with a new situation comedy for CBS, "The Lucy Show," which cast her as Lucy Carmichael, a widow with two children who shares her home with her best friend, Vivian Bagley, and Viv's son. A prime-time favorite from the start, "The Lucy Show" ran for six years.

In 1962 Lucy also took over the reins at Desilu, becoming the first woman president of a Hollywood production company. Five years later she sold Desilu to Gulf & Western and formed Lucille Ball Productions, which produced her fourth television series, "Here's Lucy," beginning in 1968. The show was quite a family affair, with Lucy's real-life children, Lucie and Desi Jr., playing her TV children; her second husband, Gary Morton, serving as executive producer; and her cousin Cleo Smith later coming on board as producer. Like her other sitcoms, "Here's Lucy" often showcased special guest stars, including Elizabeth Taylor, Johnny Carson, Liberace, Helen Hayes, and Ginger Rogers.

Lucille Ball retired from weekly series television in 1974, but during the next three years she developed and starred in a number of Lucille Ball specials. She also continued to make guest appearances on other shows, as she had done throughout her television career. She spoke candidly of her life on a Barbara Walters special, hosted "The Best of 'Three's Company,'" and was a frequent guest on Bob Hope's numerous NBC specials. She laughed with Joan Rivers on "The Tonight Show" and teamed up with Isabel Sanford on "Body Language," a 1984 CBS game show that she adored. In 1985 she took on the poignant role of a homeless New York City bag lady in the dramatic made-for-TV movie "Stone Pillow," which earned her critical acclaim but left her in frail health. The following year she was persuaded to return to weekly series television as the star of the short-lived ABC Saturday night sitcom "Life With Lucy." Later that year Lucille Ball was honored with a Lifetime Achievement Award by the Kennedy Center for the Performing Arts.

Although this remarkable lady is no longer with us, her television shows are still seen by millions of people around the world every day; the laughter she continues to generate is her greatest legacy.

"The Lucy Show": "Lucy, the Meter Maid,"
originally broadcast November 2, 1964

Just the Facts, Ma'am

Name:	Lucille Desiree Ball
Born:	August 6, 1911 Jamestown, New York
Died:	April 26, 1989 Cedars Sinai Medical Center Los Angeles, California cardiac arrest
Parents:	Desiree Hunt Ball Henry D. Ball
Married:	♥ Desiderio Alberto (Desi) Arnaz November 30, 1940 Divorced: May 4, 1960 ♥ Gary Morton November 19, 1961
Children:	Daughter: Lucie Desiree Arnaz Son: Desiderio Alberto (Desi) Arnaz Jr.
Education:	Chautauqua Institute of Music John Murray Anderson–Robert Milton Dramatic School, New York City
Film Appearances:	Debut: *Roman Scandals* (Goldwyn, 1933) Shorts: *Three Little Pigskins* (Columbia, 1934) *Perfectly Mismatched* (Columbia, 1934) *One Live Ghost* (Columbia, 1936) *So and Sew* (RKO, 1936) See also Lucille Ball Filmography
Stage Appearances:	*Wildcat* (1961), Alvin Theater, New York Tours: United States: *Hey Diddle Diddle* (1937) United States: *Dream Girl* (1947–48) United States: vaudeville tour with Desi Arnaz (1950)

Principal Radio Appearances:	"The Jack Haley Show" (1938) "My Favorite Husband" (CBS Radio, 1948–51)
Principal Television Appearances:	"I Love Lucy" (CBS, 1951–57) "The Lucy-Desi Comedy Hour" (CBS, 1957–60) "The Lucy Show" (CBS, 1962–68) "Here's Lucy" (CBS, 1968–74) "Life with Lucy" (ABC, 1986)
Awards:	Motion Picture Daily Awards: Most Promising New Star, 1951; Best Performer, 1952; Best Comedy Team (with Desi Arnaz), 1954; Best Comedienne, 1955, 1957 Emmy Awards: Best Comedienne, 1952; Best Actress in a Continuing Performance, 1955 ("I Love Lucy"); Outstanding Continuing Performance by an Actress in a Leading Role in a Comedy Series, 1967, 1968 ("The Lucy Show") International Radio and Television Society: Gold Medal, 1971 Hollywood Women's Press Club Golden Apple Award: Star of the Year, 1973 Ruby Award, 1974 Entertainer of the Year Award, 1975 Friar's Club Life Achievement Award, 1977 Hollywood Foreign Press Association: Cecil B. De Mille Award, 1978 Television Academy Hall of Fame Inductee, 1984 Kennedy Center for the Performing Arts: Lifetime Achievement Citation, 1986 Hasty Pudding Award: Woman of the Year, 1988 Presidential Medal of Freedom (posthumously), 1989

Radio and Television Specials and Guest Appearances

Selected Radio Guest Appearances

"Good News of 1940" (NBC; December 28, 1939)

"The Campbell Playhouse" (CBS; February 18, 1940)

"The Gulf Screen Guild Theatre: 'Tight Shoes'" (CBS; April 12, 1942)

"The Kraft Music Hall" (NBC; April 1, 1943)

"Duffy's Tavern" (NBC Blue; September 12, 1943)

"Suspense: 'A Little Piece of Rope'" (CBS; October 14, 1943)

"The Abbott and Costello Show" (NBC; November 11, 1943)

"Suspense: 'Dime a Dance'" (CBS; January 13, 1944)

"The Kraft Music Hall" (NBC; March 2, 1944)

"Suspense: 'The Ten Grand'" (CBS; June 22, 1944)

"The Lux Radio Theatre" (CBS; September 25, 1944)

"The Lady Esther Screen Guild Players: 'A Girl, a Guy, and a Gob'" (NBC; October 9, 1944)

"The Lady Esther Screen Guild Players: 'China Seas'" (NBC; December 4, 1944)

"Suspense: 'A Shroud for Sarah'" (CBS; October 25, 1945)

"The Colgate Sports Newsreel" (NBC; May 24, 1946)

"The Radio Reader's Digest: 'The Whirligig of Life'" (CBS; June 9, 1946)

"The Radio Reader's Digest: 'The Lion and the Mousey'" (CBS; May 22, 1947)

"Hollywood Fights Back" (ABC; October 26, 1947)

"The Jimmy Durante Show" (NBC; October 29, 1947)

"The Lux Radio Theatre: 'The Dark Corner'" (CBS; November 10, 1947)

"The Kraft Music Hall" (NBC; January 22, 1948)

"The Jimmy Durante Show" (NBC; April 28, 1948)

"The Cavalcade of America: 'Skylark Song'" (NBC; June 21, 1948)

"Erskine Johnson's Hollywood Story" (Mutual; August 25, 1948)

"Screen Directors' Playhouse: 'Her Husband's Affairs'" (NBC; May 22, 1949)

"The Bob Hope Swan Show" (NBC; May 31, 1949)

"Suspense: 'Red-headed Woman'" (CBS; November 17, 1949)

"Screen Directors' Playhouse: 'Miss Grant Takes Richmond'" (NBC; May 19, 1950)

"The Cavalcade of America: 'The Redemption of Lottie Moon'" (NBC; June 13, 1950)

"Screen Directors' Playhouse: 'A Foreign Affair'" (NBC; March 1, 1951)

"Screen Directors' Playhouse: 'Bachelor Mother'" (NBC; March 8, 1951)

"The Lux Radio Theatre: 'Fancy Pants'" (CBS; September 10, 1951)

Selected Television Specials and Guest Appearances

"Show of the Year" (NBC; June 10, 1950)

"The Bob Hope Show" (NBC; September 14, 1950)

"What's My Line?" (NBC; February 21, 1954)

"The Bob Hope Show" (NBC; November 18, 1956)

"Desilu Playhouse: 'K. O. Kitty'" (CBS; November 17, 1958)

"Make Room for Daddy: 'Lucy Upsets the Williams' Household'" (CBS; January 5, 1959)

"The Ann Sothern Show: 'The Lucy Story'" (CBS; October 5, 1959)

"The Milton Berle Special" (NBC; November 1, 1959)

"The Desilu Playhouse: 'The Desilu Review'" (CBS; December 25, 1959)

"Hedda Hopper's Hollywood" (NBC; January 10, 1960)

"Bob Hope Sports Awards" (NBC; February 15, 1961)

"The Good Years" (CBS; January 12, 1962)

"The Bob Hope Show" (NBC; October 24, 1962)

"The Greatest Show on Earth: 'Lady in Limbo'" (ABC; December 10, 1963)

"Lucille Ball Comedy Hour" (CBS; April 19, 1964)

"The Jack Benny Program: 'The Lucille Ball Show'" (NBC; October 2, 1964)

"Bob Hope Chrysler Theatre: 'Have Girls, Will Travel'" (NBC; October 16, 1964)

"A Salute to Stan Laurel" (CBS; November 23, 1965)

"A Bob Hope Comedy Special" (NBC; September 28, 1966)

"Lucy in London" (CBS; October 24, 1966)

"Carol Plus Two" (CBS; January 15, 1967)

"The Ed Sullivan Show" (CBS; March 17, 1968)

"The Jack Benny Special" (NBC; March 20, 1968)

"Jack Benny's Birthday Special" (NBC; February 17, 1969)

"Dinah Shore Special" (NBC; April 13, 1969)

"From Hollywood with Love: The Ann-Margret Special"
(CBS; December 6, 1969)
"The Bob Hope Show" (NBC; November 16, 1970)
"Jack Benny's 20th TV Anniversary" (NBC;
November 16, 1970)
"Super Comedy Bowl" (CBS; January 10, 1971)
"Make Room for Grand Daddy" (ABC; January 21, 1971)
"Everything You Always Wanted to Know about Jack Benny—
but Were Afraid to Ask" (NBC; March 10, 1971)
"Swing Out, Sweet Land" (NBC; April 8, 1971)
"A Salute to TV's 25th Anniversary" (ABC;
September 10, 1972)
"Steve and Eydie . . . On Stage" (NBC; September 16, 1973)
"The Bob Hope Show" (NBC; December 9, 1973)
"Happy Anniversary and Goodbye" (CBS; November 19, 1974)
"Dean Martin Celebrity Roast: Lucille Ball" (NBC;
February 7, 1975)
"A Lucille Ball Special Starring Lucille Ball and Dean
Martin" (CBS; March 1, 1975)
"The 27th Annual Emmy Awards" (CBS; May 19, 1975)
"A Lucille Ball Special: Three for Two" (CBS;
December 3, 1975)
"Shirley MacLaine Special: Gypsy in My Soul" (CBS;
January 20, 1976)
"A Lucille Ball Special: What Now, Catherine Curtis?"
(CBS; March 30, 1976)
"Texaco Presents Bob Hope's World of Comedy" (NBC;
October 29, 1976)
"CBS Salutes Lucy: The First 25 Years" (CBS;
November 28, 1976)
"Dean Martin Celebrity Roast: Danny Thomas" (NBC;
December 15, 1976)
"Texaco Presents Bob Hope's All-Star Comedy Tribute to
Vaudeville" (NBC; March 25, 1977)
"The Lucille Ball Special" (CBS; November 21, 1977)
"The Second Annual Circus of the Stars" (CBS;
December 5, 1977)
"The Barbara Walters Special" (ABC; December 6, 1977)
"The Fabulous '50's" (NBC; March 5, 1978)
"Gene Kelly—An American in Pasadena" (CBS;
March 13, 1978)
"The American Film Institute Salute to Henry Fonda"
(CBS; March 15, 1978)
"A Tribute to 'Mr. Television,' Milton Berle" (NBC;
March 26, 1978)
"CBS: On the Air" (CBS; March 27, 1978)
"Dean Martin Celebrity Roast: Jimmy Stewart" (NBC;
May 10, 1978)
"Happy Birthday, Bob" (NBC; May 29, 1978)
"General Electric All-Star Anniversary" (ABC;
September 29, 1978)
"Lucy Comes to Nashville" (CBS; November 19,
1978)
"The Mary Tyler Moore Hour" (CBS; March 4,
1979)

"Lucy Moves to NBC" (NBC; February 8, 1980)
"The Best of 'Three's Company'" (ABC; May 18, 1982)
"Bob Hope on the Road to Hollywood" (NBC; March 2, 1983)
"Happy Birthday, Bob" (NBC; May 23, 1983)
"The Television Academy Hall of Fame" (NBC: March 4, 1984)
"Bob Hope's Who Makes the World Laugh, Part 2"
(NBC; April 4, 1984)
"Body Language" (CBS; September 10–14, 1984)
"The Tonight Show" (NBC; December 3, 1984)
"All-Star Party for Lucille Ball" (CBS; December 9, 1984)
"Body Language" (CBS; December 24, 26–28, 1984)
"Bob Hope Buys NBC" (NBC; September 17, 1985)
"The Tonight Show" (NBC; November 1, 1985)
"Stone Pillow" (CBS; November 5, 1985)
"The Late Show Starring Joan Rivers" (FOX;
October 30, 1986)
"The 9th Annual Kennedy Center Honors" (CBS;
December 26, 1986)
"Happy Birthday Hollywood" (ABC; May 18, 1987)
"The 10th Annual Kennedy Center Honors" (CBS;
December 30, 1987)
"America's Tribute to Bob Hope" (NBC; March 5, 1988)
"Happy Birthday, Bob" (NBC; May 16, 1988)
"Super Password" (NBC; November 7–11, 1988)
"Sixty-First Annual Academy Awards" (ABC;
March 29, 1989)

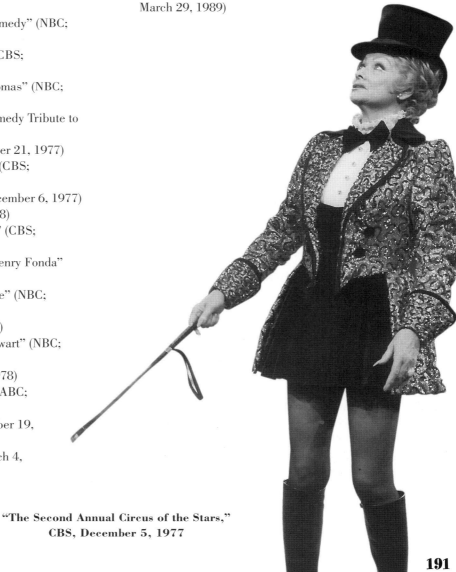

**"The Second Annual Circus of the Stars,"
CBS, December 5, 1977**

191

"My Favorite Husband"

CBS Radio
Situation Comedy
30 Minutes
125 Episodes
Debuted: July 5, 1948
Ended: March 31, 1951

Format I
(July 5, 1948-December 26, 1948)
Liz Cugat: Lucille Ball
George Cugat: Richard Denning*
Katy (the Cugats' maid): Ruth Perrott
Cory Cartwright: John Heistand**

Format II
(January 7, 1949-March 31, 1951)
Liz Cooper: Lucille Ball
George Cooper: Richard Denning
Katy (the Coopers' maid): Ruth Perrott
Rudolph Atterbury (George's boss and friend): Gale Gordon
Iris Atterbury (Rudolph's wife, Liz's friend): Bea Benaderet

Producers: Jess Oppenheimer, Gordon T. Hughes (1948), Harry Ackerman (1948)
Directors: Jess Oppenheimer, Gordon T. Hughes (1948), Harry Ackerman (1948)
Writers: Jess Oppenheimer, Bob Carroll, Jr., Madelyn Pugh, Bill Davenport (1948), Frank Fox (1948), John Michael Hayes (1948), Ben Gersham (1948), Jack Crutcher (1948), Martin Weiner (1948), Phil Cole (1948)
Original Music: Marlin Skiles
Music Conductor: Wilbur Hatch
Sponsor: sustaining (1948), Jell-O (General Foods) (1949–51)

*Lee Bowman portrayed George Cugat in the Special Preview Program on July 5, 1948. He was replaced by Richard Denning when the show began as a weekly series on July 23.
**Hal March played the role of Cory Cartwright in the episodes from July 5–July 30, 1948.

♥   ♥   ♥

The "My Favorite Husband" Story, Format I

When George and Liz Cugat got married, he was the town's most eligible bachelor; she, its most beautiful debutante. But that was ten years ago and by now they are just like all the other married couples in town. Whether they're spending time with their friends, adapting to their respective mothers-in-law, or coping with the resurgence of old flames, Liz and George are definitely each other's favorite.

♥   ♥   ♥

The "My Favorite Husband" Story, Format II

There's never a dull moment in the little white two-story house where George and Liz Cooper live. While George is at work at the bank, Liz keeps busy trying to balance her household account, babysitting to earn extra money, and scheming to convince her husband to buy her a new Easter outfit. George's boss is bank president Rudolph Atterbury. Rudolph's wife, Iris, is Liz's best friend. Together, the two couples enjoy the many misadventures of married life.

Head writer Jess Oppenheimer (left), Lucille Ball, and
Richard Denning rehearse an episode of "My Favorite Husband."

♥   ♥   ♥

"My Favorite Husband" Trivia

♥ "My Favorite Husband" was based on the book *Mr. and Mrs. Cugat* by Isabel Scott Rorick.

♥ Liz Cooper's maiden name is Elliott.

♥ George and Liz Cooper live at 321 Bundy Drive in Sheridan Falls.

♥ The Bundy Drive address was chosen after "My Favorite Husband" head writer Jess Oppenheimer and his wife bought a home on Bundy Drive in Brentwood, California, in 1948.

♥ Before Gale Gordon took on the role of Rudolph Atterbury, the character was played by Joe Kearns (episode 23, "Liz's New Dress.")

♥ Gale Gordon first appeared as Rudolph Atterbury in episode 35, "Charity Review," on March 11, 1949. Two weeks later, Bea Benaderet premiered in her role as Rudolph's wife, Iris.

♥ When the series changed format in January 1949, Jell-O was secured as sponsor.

♥ Although some later episodes have the same titles as earlier ones, the later programs are either revised versions of the earlier shows or completely different.

♥ Only one episode of "My Favorite Husband" was rebroadcast. "Liz Changes Her Mind" first aired on June 24, 1949; it aired again on September 30, 1950.

♥ Jean VanderPyl (the voice of Wilma Flintstone) and Doris Singleton (Carolyn Appleby on "I Love Lucy") were supporting players in select "My Favorite Husband" episodes.

♥   ♥   ♥

"My Favorite Husband" Episode Titles and Original Air Dates

Special Preview Program (The Cugats' Tenth Wedding Anniversary) (7/5/48)

1. Untitled (Literary Club's Speaker Comes to Dinner) (7/23/48)
2. Untitled (The Magazine Photographer) (7/30/48)
3. Untitled (The Portrait Painter) (8/6/48)
4. Untitled (The Kissing Booth) (8/13/48)
5. "Liz Teaches the Samba" (8/20/48)
6. Untitled (Is Your Ship of Matrimony on the Rocks?) (8/27/48)
7. Untitled (Liz's Mother Has Second Thoughts) (9/3/48)
8. Untitled (The Swami) (9/10/48)
9. Untitled (Making Friends with General Timberlake) (9/17/48)
10. Untitled (Knitting Baby Booties) (9/24/48)
11. "Young Matron League Tryouts" (10/2/48)
12. Untitled (The Cugats' Tenth Wedding Anniversary) (10/3/48)
13. Untitled (Young Matrons' League Game) (10/9/48)

14. "Liz Sells Dresses" (10/16/48)
15. "Quiz Show" (10/23/48)
16. "The Election" (10/30/48)
17. "Katy and Roscoe" (11/6/48)
18. "Learning to Drive" (11/13/48)
19. "George Attends a Teen-age Dance" (11/20/48)
20. "Is There a Baby in the House?" (11/27/48)
21. "Be Your Husband's Best Friend" (12/4/48)
22. "Respective Mustaches" (12/11/48)
23. "Liz's New Dress" (12/18/48)
24. "Numerology" (12/25/48)
25. "Young Matrons' League Tryouts" (12/26/48)
26. "Over Budget—Beans" (1/7/49)
27. "Piano and Violin Lessons" (1/14/49)
28. "Marriage License" (1/21/49)
29. "Absolute Truth" (1/28/49)
30. "Speech for Civic Organization" (2/4/49)
31. "Valentine's Day" (2/11/49)
32. "Secretarial School" (2/18/49)
33. "Absentmindedness" (2/25/49)
34. "Mother-in-Law" (3/4/49)
35. "Charity Review" (3/11/49)
36. "Giveaway Program" (3/18/49)
37. "Old Jokes and Old Stories" (3/25/49)
38. "April Fool's Day" (4/1/49)
39. "Gum Machine" (4/8/49)
40. "Horseback Riding" (4/15/49)
41. "Time Budgeting" (4/22/49)
42. "Vacation Time" (4/29/49)
43. "Overweight" (5/6/49)
44. "Anniversary Presents" (5/13/49)
45. "Getting Old" (5/20/49)
46. "Liz in the Hospital" (5/27/49)
47. "Budget—Mr. Atterbury" (6/3/49)
48. "Hair Dyed" (6/10/49)
49. "Television" (6/17/49)
50. "Liz Changes Her Mind" (6/24/49)
51. "Reminiscing" (7/1/49)
52. "The Elves" (9/2/49)
53. "The Auction" (9/9/49)
54. "Baseball" (9/16/49)
55. "The Attic" (9/23/49)
56. "Women's Club Election" (9/30/49)
57. "George Tries for a Raise" (10/7/49)
58. "Television" (10/14/49)
59. "Superstition" (10/21/49)
60. "Halloween Surprise Party" (10/28/49)
61. "Mother-in-Law" (11/4/49)
62. "Baby Sitting" (11/11/49)
63. "Katy and Mr. Negley" (11/18/49)
64. "Quiz Show" (11/25/49)
65. "College Homecoming" (12/2/49)
66. "The French Lessons" (12/9/49)
67. "George's Christmas Present" (12/16/49)
68. "The Sleigh Ride" (12/23/49)
69. "Liz and George Handcuffed" (12/30/49)

70. "The Question of Another Woman" (1/6/50)
71. "Liz Teaches Iris to Drive" (1/13/50)
72. "Liz and the Green Wig" (1/20/50)
73. "Liz Writes a Song" (1/27/50)
74. "The Country Club Dance" (2/3/50)
75. "Mrs. Cooper's Boyfriend" (2/10/50)
76. "Liz Teaches the Samba" (2/17/50)
77. "Liz Redecorates the House" (2/24/50)
78. "Women's Rights, Part 1" (3/5/50)
79. "Women's Rights, Part 2" (3/12/50)
80. "The Wills" (3/19/50)
81. "Liz's Radio Script" (3/26/50)
82. "April Fool" (4/2/50)
83. "Hobbies" (4/9/50)
84. "Anniversary" (4/16/50)
85. "Liz Appears on Television" (4/23/50)
86. "Spring Housecleaning" (4/30/50)
87. "The Health Farm" (5/7/50)
88. "Numerology" (5/14/50)
89. "Mrs. Cooper Thinks Liz Is Pregnant" (5/21/50)
90. "Selling Dresses" (5/28/50)
91. "George Is Messy" (6/4/50)
92. "Liz Learns to Swim" (6/11/50)
93. "Be a Pal" (6/18/50)
94. "Dancing Lessons" (6/25/50)
95. "Husbands Are Sloppy Dressers" (9/2/50)
96. "Gossip" (9/9/50)
97. "Movies" (9/16/50)
98. "Fuller Brush Show" (9/23/50)
99. "Liz Becomes a Sculptress" (10/7/50)
100. "Liz Cooks Dinner for Twelve" (10/14/50)
101. "Safety Drive" (10/21/50)
102. "The Football Game" (10/28/50)
103. "The Two Mrs. Coopers" (11/4/50)
104. "Vacation from Marriage" (11/11/50)
105. "Liz Goes to Night School" (11/18/50)
106. "Liz's Birthday" (11/25/50)
107. "Trying to Marry off Peggy Martin" (12/2/50)
108. "Trying to Cash the Prize Check" (12/9/50)
109. "The Christmas Cards" (12/16/50)
110. "The Christmas Stag" (12/23/50)
111. "Liz Has the Flimjabs" (12/30/50)
112. "Liz Substitutes in Club Play" (1/6/51)
113. "The Cuckoo Clock" (1/13/51)
114. "Liz Stretches the Truth" (1/20/51)
115. "George Is Drafted—Liz's Baby" (1/27/51)
116. "Liz's Inferiority Complex" (2/3/51)
117. "The Misunderstanding of the Black Eye" (2/10/51)
118. "Renewal of Driver's License" (2/17/51)
119. "The Two Mothers-in-Law" (2/24/51)
120. "The Passports" (3/3/51)
121. "The Surprise Party" (3/10/51)
122. "Liz Hires a New Secretary for George" (3/17/51)
123. "Iris and Liz's Easter" (3/24/51)
124. "The April Fool Joke" (3/31/51)

"I Love Lucy"

CBS
Situation Comedy
30 Minutes
181 Episodes
Debuted: October 15, 1951
Left prime time: June 24, 1957

Cast

Lucy Ricardo: Lucille Ball
Ricky Ricardo (Lucy's husband; a bandleader): Desi Arnaz
Ethel Mertz (friend and landlady): Vivian Vance
Fred Mertz (friend and landlord): William Frawley
Baby Ricky Ricardo (January 19, 1953, episode): James J. Gouzer
Baby Ricky Ricardo (April 20, 1953, episode): Richard Lee Simmons, Ronald Lee Simmons
Baby Ricky Ricardo: Joseph D. Mayer, Michael L. Mayer
Little Ricky Ricardo (the Ricardos' son; 1956–57): Richard Keith

Occasional Cast

Matilda Trumbull (the Ricardos' neighbor): Elizabeth Patterson
Jerry (Ricky's agent): Jerry Hausner
Alvin Littlefield (owner of the Tropicana): Gale Gordon
Phoebe Littlefield (Alvin's wife): Bea Benaderet
Marion Strong (Lucy's friend): Shirley Mitchell
Caroline Appleby (Lucy's friend): Doris Singleton
Charley Appleby (Carolyn's husband) : Hy Averback
Mrs. McGillicuddy (Lucy's mother): Kathryn Card
Betty Ramsey (Lucy's Westport neighbor): Mary Jane Croft
Ralph Ramsey (Betty's husband): Frank Nelson

Staff

Executive Producer: Desi Arnaz
Producer: Jess Oppenheimer (1951–56), Desi Arnaz (1956–57)
Directors: Mark Daniels (1951–53), William Asher (1952–57), James V. Kern (1955–57)
Writers: Jess Oppenheimer (1951–56), Madelyn Pugh, Bob Carroll, Jr., Bob Weiskopf (1955–57), Bob Schiller (1955–57)
Music Conductor: Wilbur Hatch
Music: The Desi Arnaz Orchestra
Music Composer: Eliot Daniel
Director of Photography: Karl "Papa" Freund (1951–56), Robert de Grasse (1956), Sid Hickox (1956–57)
Announcer: Johnny Jacobs
Makeup: Max Factor, Hal King
Sponsors: Philip Morris Cigarettes (1951–55), Procter & Gamble (1954–57), General Foods (1955–57), Ford Motor Company (1956–57)

♥ ♥ ♥

The "I Love Lucy" Story

Cuban-born bandleader Ricky Ricardo and his wife, Lucy, live in a brownstone apartment building on East 68th Street in New York City. The beautiful but daffy Lucy has the habit of getting herself into jams, scrapes, and predicaments of all kinds. The Ricardos' best friends and landlords, Fred and Ethel Mertz, frequently find themselves in the middle of Lucy's outlandish escapades, whether she's plotting to land a part in her husband's nightclub act, determined to write her first novel, or concocting a surefire get-rich-quick scheme.

After Lucy gives birth to their only child, Little Ricky, and Ricky achieves great success as an entertainer, Ricky is asked to go to Hollywood to star in his first motion picture. Together, the Ricardos and Mertzes drive to California for Ricky's big break. Along the way, they are held at gunpoint when they try to flee a rundown motel, square dance their way out of a Tennessee jail, and put on a benefit show for Ethel's hometown friends in Albuquerque.

Once in Hollywood, star-struck Lucy spills a tray of desserts on William Holden, gets trapped inside John Wayne's dressing room, and wrestles with a dog guarding Richard Widmark's estate. By the time Ricky finishes his movie, Lucy has developed quite a reputation, and all of Hollywood is relieved to learn the redheaded dynamo is on her way home.

Shortly after the Ricardos return to New York, the Ricky Ricardo Orchestra is booked for an extensive European tour, and Lucy, Ricky, Ethel, and Fred soon find themselves visiting England, France, Switzerland and Italy, where Lucy ends up barefoot in a vat—stomping grapes at a small vineyard.

Back in the States, Lucy and Ricky decide to move to the country so Little Ricky can enjoy the benefits of "clean, fresh air and home-grown foods." The Ricardos break the news to Fred and Ethel and buy a home in Westport, Connecticut. But the Ricardos and Mertzes can't stay apart for long, and soon Fred and Ethel relocate to Westport, renting the Ricardos' guest house. With the Mertzes close by, Lucy grows tulips that melt in the sun, learns all about how not to raise chickens, battles with a runaway lawn mower, and experiences many other joys that country life has to offer.

♥   ♥   ♥

"I Love Lucy" Trivia

♥ Lucy's maiden name is McGillicuddy; her middle name is Esmeralda.
♥ The Ricardos' New York address: 623 East 68th Street, New York City.
♥ The Ricardos move from apartment 4A to 3B in episode 61. In episode 72, however, Lucy claims to live in 3D.
♥ Ricky worked at the Tropicana before owning his own nightclub, Club Babalu.
♥ Ricky has five brothers.

♥ Ethel's middle name is Mae, Roberta, or Louise (depending on the episode).
♥ Fred is from Steubenville, Ohio, and his middle name is Hobart.
♥ Lucy and Ricky buy their Connecticut home from Eleanor and Joe Spaulding.
♥ Butch is the Mertzes' dog, and is only seen in episode 4, "The Diet."
♥ Ethel's father is Will Potter.

♥   ♥   ♥

"I Love Lucy" Episode Titles and Original Air Dates

1. "Lucy Thinks Ricky is Trying to Murder Her" (11/5/51)
2. "The Girls Want to Go to a Nightclub" (10/15/51)
3. "Be A Pal" (10/22/51)
4. "The Diet" (10/29/51)
5. "The Quiz Show" (11/12/51)
6. "The Audition" (11/19/51)
7. "The Seance" (11/26/51)
8. "Men Are Messy" (12/3/51)
9. "Drafted" (12/24/51)
10. "The Fur Coat" (12/10/51)
11. "Lucy Is Jealous of Girl Singer" (12/17/51)
12. "The Adagio" (12/31/51)
13. "The Benefit" (1/7/52)
14. "The Amateur Hour" (1/14/52)
15. "Lucy Plays Cupid" (1/21/52)
16. "Lucy Fakes Illness" (1/28/52)
17. "Lucy Writes a Play" (2/4/52)
18. "Breaking the Lease" (2/11/52)
19. "The Ballet" (2/18/52)
20. "The Young Fans" (2/25/52)
21. "New Neighbors" (3/3/52)
22. "Fred And Ethel Fight" (3/10/52)
23. "The Mustache" (3/17/52)
24. "The Gossip" (3/24/52)
25. "Pioneer Women" (3/31/52)
26. "The Marriage License" (4/7/52)
27. "The Kleptomaniac" (4/14/52)
28. "Cuban Pals" (4/21/52)
29. "The Freezer" (4/28/52)
30. "Lucy Does a TV Commercial" (5/5/52)
31. "The Publicity Agent" (5/12/52)
32. "Lucy Gets Ricky on the Radio" (5/19/52)
33. "Lucy's Schedule" (5/26/52)
34. "Ricky Thinks He's Getting Bald" (6/2/52)
35. "Ricky Asks for a Raise" (6/9/52)
36. "Anniversary Present" (9/29/52)
37. "The Handcuffs" (10/6/52)
38. "The Operetta" (10/13/52)
39. "Job Switching" (9/15/52)
40. "The Saxophone" (9/22/52)
41. "Vacation from Marriage" (10/27/52)
42. "The Courtroom" (11/10/52)
43. "Redecorating" (11/24/52)
44. "Ricky Loses His Voice" (12/1/52)
45. "Sales Resistance" (1/26/53)
46. "Inferiority Complex" (2/2/53)
47. "The Club Election" (2/16/53)
48. "The Black Eye" (3/9/53)
49. "Lucy Changes Her Mind" (3/30/53)
50. "Lucy Is Enceinte" (12/8/52)
51. "Pregnant Women Are Unpredictable" (12/15/52)
52. "Lucy's Show Biz Swan Song" (12/22/52)
53. "Lucy Hires an English Tutor" (12/29/52)
54. "Ricky Has Labor Pains" (1/5/53)

**From the original animated opening credits of
"I Love Lucy," 1951**

55. "Lucy Becomes a Sculptress" (1/12/53)
56. "Lucy Goes to the Hospital" (1/19/53)
57. "No Children Allowed" (4/20/53)
58. "Lucy Hires a Maid" (4/27/53)
59. "The Indian Show" (5/4/53)
60. "Lucy's Last Birthday" (5/11/53)
61. "Ricardos Change Apartments" (5/18/53)
62. "Lucy Is Matchmaker" (5/25/53)
63. "Lucy Wants New Furniture" (6/1/53)
64. "The Camping Trip" (6/8/53)
65. "Ricky's Life Story" (10/5/53)
66. "Ricky and Fred Are TV Fans" (6/22/53)
67. "Never Do Business with Friends" (6/29/53)
68. "The Girls Go into Business" (10/12/53)
69. "Lucy and Ethel Buy the Same Dress" (10/19/53)
70. "Equal Rights" (10/26/53)
71. "Baby Pictures" (11/2/53)
72. "Lucy Tells the Truth" (11/9/53)
73. "The French Revue" (11/16/53)
74. "Redecorating the Mertzes' Apartment" (11/23/53)
75. "Too Many Crooks" (11/30/53)
76. "Changing the Boys' Wardrobe" (12/7/53)
77. "Lucy Has Her Eyes Examined" (12/14/53)
78. "Ricky's Old Girlfriend" (12/21/53)
79. "The Million Dollar Idea" (1/11/54)
80. "Ricky Minds the Baby" (1/18/54)
81. "Charm School" (1/25/54)

82. "Sentimental Anniversary" (2/1/54)
83. "Fan Magazine Interview" (2/8/54)
84. "Oil Wells" (2/15/54)
85. "Ricky Loses His Temper" (2/22/54)
86. "Home Movies" (3/1/54)
87. "Bonus Bucks" (3/8/54)
88. "Ricky's Hawaiian Vacation" (3/22/54)
89. "Lucy Is Envious" (3/29/54)
90. "Lucy Writes a Novel" (4/5/54)
91. "The Club Dance" (4/12/54)
92. "The Diner" (4/26/54)
93. "The Black Wig" (4/19/54)
94. "Tennessee Ernie Visits" (5/3/54)
95. "Tennessee Ernie Hangs On" (5/10/54)
96. "The Golf Game" (5/17/54)
97. "The Sublease" (5/24/54)
98. "Lucy Cries Wolf" (10/18/54)
99. "The Matchmaker" (10/25/54)
100. "The Business Manager" (10/4/54)
101. "Mr. and Mrs. TV Show" (4/11/55)
102. "Mertz And Kurtz" (10/11/54)
103. "Ricky's Movie Offer" (11/8/54)
104. "Ricky's Screen Test" (11/15/54)
105. "Lucy's Mother-In-Law" (11/22/54)
106. "Ethel's Birthday" (11/29/54)
107. "Ricky's Contract" (12/6/54)
108. "Getting Ready" (12/13/54)

109. "Lucy Learns to Drive" (1/3/55)
110. "California, Here We Come" (1/10/55)
111. "First Stop" (1/17/55)
112. "Tennessee Bound" (1/24/55)
113. "Ethel's Hometown" (1/31/55)
114. "L.A. at Last" (2/7/55)
115. "Don Juan and the Starlets" (2/14/55)
116. "Lucy Gets in Pictures" (2/21/55)
117. "The Fashion Show" (2/28/55)
118. "The Hedda Hopper Show" (3/14/55)
119. "Don Juan Is Shelved" (3/21/55)
120. "Bull Fight Dance" (3/28/55)
121. "Hollywood Anniversary" (4/4/55)
122. "The Star Upstairs" (4/18/55)
123. "In Palm Springs" (4/25/55)
124. "Harpo Marx" (5/9/55)
125. "Dancing Star" (5/2/55)
126. "Ricky Needs an Agent" (5/16/55)
127. "The Tour" (5/30/55)
128. "Lucy Visits Grauman's" (10/3/55)
129. "Lucy and John Wayne" (10/10/55)
130. "Lucy and the Dummy" (10/17/55)
131. "Ricky Sells the Car" (10/24/55)
132. "The Great Train Robbery" (10/31/55)
133. "Homecoming" (11/7/55)
134. "Person to Person" (11/14/55)
135. "Lucy Goes to a Rodeo" (11/28/55)
136. "Nursery School" (12/5/55)
137. "Ricky's European Booking" (12/12/55)
138. "The Passports" (12/19/55)
139. "Staten Island Ferry" (1/2/56)
140. "Bon Voyage" (1/16/56)
141. "Lucy's Second Honeymoon" (1/23/56)
142. "Lucy Meets the Queen" (1/30/56)
143. "The Fox Hunt" (2/6/56)
144. "Lucy Goes to Scotland" (2/20/56)
145. "Paris at Last" (2/27/56)
146. "Lucy Meets Charles Boyer" (3/5/56)
147. "Lucy Gets a Paris Gown" (3/19/56)

148. "Lucy in the Swiss Alps" (3/26/56)
149. "Lucy Gets Homesick" (4/9/56)
150. "Lucy's Italian Movie" (4/16/56)
151. "Lucy's Bicycle Trip" (4/23/56)
152. "Lucy Goes to Monte Carlo" (5/7/56)
153. "Home from Europe" (5/14/56)
154. "Lucy and Bob Hope" (10/1/56)
155. "Lucy Meets Orson Welles" (10/15/56)
156. "Little Ricky Gets Stage Fright" (10/22/56)
157. "Little Ricky Learns to Play the Drums" (10/8/56)
158. "Visitor from Italy" (10/29/56)
159. "Off to Florida" (11/12/56)
160. "Deep Sea Fishing" (11/19/56)
161. "Desert Island" (11/26/56)
162. "Ricardos Visit Cuba" (12/3/56)
163. "Little Ricky's School Pageant" (12/17/56)
164. "Lucy and the Loving Cup" (1/7/57)
165. "Little Ricky Gets a Dog" (1/21/57)
166. "Lucy and Superman" (1/14/57)
167. "Lucy Wants to Move to the Country" (1/28/57)
168. "Lucy Hates to Leave" (2/4/57)
169. "Lucy Misses the Mertzes" (2/11/57)
170. "Lucy Gets Chummy with the Neighbors" (2/18/57)
171. "Lucy Raises Chickens" (3/4/57)
172. "Lucy Does the Tango" (3/11/57)
173. "Ragtime Band" (3/18/57)
174. "Lucy's Night in Town" (3/25/57)
175. "Housewarming" (4/1/57)
176. "Building a Barbecue" (4/8/57)
177. "The Country Club Dance" (4/22/57)
178. "Lucy Raises Tulips" (4/29/57)
179. "The Ricardos Dedicate a Statue" (5/6/57)
180. "The 'I Love Lucy' Christmas Show" (12/24/56)
181. Pilot*

*The "I Love Lucy" pilot served as the show's "screen test" and was not televised during the series' initial run. "Lost" for years, the pilot was rediscovered and broadcast as a CBS special, "I Love Lucy: The Very First Show" on April 30, 1990.

"The Lucy-Desi Comedy Hour"

Original Title: "The Lucille Ball–Desi Arnaz Show"
CBS
Situation Comedy
60 Minutes
13 Episodes
Debuted: November 6, 1957
Left prime time: April 1, 1960

Cast

Lucy Ricardo: Lucille Ball
Ricky Ricardo: Desi Arnaz
Ethel Mertz: Vivian Vance
Fred Mertz: William Frawley
Little Ricky: Richard Keith

Staff

Executive Producer: Desi Arnaz
Producer: Bert Granet
Associate Producer: Jack Aldworth
Director: Jerry Thorpe (1957–59), Desi Arnaz (1959–60)
Writers: Bob Carroll, Jr., Madelyn Martin, Bob Schiller, Bob Weiskopf
Music: Wilbur Hatch
Director of Photography: Sid Hickox, Nick Musuraca (1959)
Makeup: Hal King
Sponsors: Ford Motor Company (1957–58), Westinghouse Electric Company (1958–60)

♥   ♥   ♥

"The Lucy-Desi Comedy Hour" Story

Although they live in Connecticut, Lucy and Ricky Ricardo are often on the go—traveling wherever Ricky's career might take him. With their friends Fred and Ethel, the Ricardos hunt for uranium in Nevada, create havoc at the Mexican border, and find themselves without hotel accommodations in Alaska, where Lucy is forced to spend a night on a very uncooperative hammock. When Ricky's band is booked for an engagement in Tokyo, the Ricardos and the Mertzes travel to Japan; it isn't long before Lucy finds herself swimming with a fish and impersonating a geisha girl in an attempt to own a strand of real pearls.

Back at home, Lucy Ricardo is never bored. When she's not fighting with her famous next-door neighbor, Tallulah Bankhead, she can be found plotting to get Milton Berle to appear in a PTA benefit show, falling asleep in a bowl of cereal on live television, trying to hide a race horse in the house, and spending a day in court after a snowball fight gets a little out of hand.

From the animated opening credits of
"The Lucy-Desi Comedy Hour"

♥   ♥   ♥

"The Lucy-Desi Comedy Hour" Trivia

♥ The premiere episode of "The Lucy-Desi Comedy Hour" ran 75 minutes.

♥ The original opening scene in the episode "Lucy Takes a Cruise to Havana" found gossip columnist Hedda Hopper asking Lucy how she met Ricky. This introductory scene was cut when the show went into syndication.

♥ Tallulah Bankhead's role in the episode "The Celebrity Next Door" was originally intended for Bette Davis.

♥ During the filming of "The Celebrity Next Door" Desi finalized the purchase of RKO Studios for Desilu.

♥ During the 1958–59 season, "The Lucy-Desi Comedy Hour" became part of "The Desilu Playhouse," an anthology series featuring a variety of television productions from Desilu Studios.

♥ "Lucy Goes to Alaska" was filmed on location in Lake Arrowhead, California.

♥   ♥   ♥

"The Lucy-Desi Comedy Hour" Episode Titles and Original Air Dates

1. "Lucy Takes a Cruise to Havana" (11/6/57)
2. "The Celebrity Next Door" (12/3/57)
3. "Lucy Hunts Uranium" (1/3/58)
4. "Lucy Wins a Race Horse" (2/3/58)
5. "Lucy Goes to Sun Valley" (4/14/58)
6. "Lucy Goes to Mexico" (10/6/58)
7. "Lucy Makes Room for Danny" (12/1/58)
8. "Lucy Goes to Alaska" (2/9/59)
9. "Lucy Wants a Career" (4/13/59)
10. "Lucy's Summer Vacation" (6/8/59)
11. "Milton Berle Hides out at the Ricardos" (9/25/59)
12. "The Ricardos Go to Japan" (11/27/59)
13. "Lucy Meets the Mustache" (4/1/60)

"The Lucy Show"

CBS
Situation Comedy
30 Minutes
156 Episodes
Debuted: October 1, 1962
Left prime time: September 16, 1968

Cast

Lucy Carmichael: Lucille Ball
Vivian Bagley: Vivian Vance
Chris Carmichael (Lucy's daughter): Candy Moore
Jerry Carmichael (Lucy's son): Jimmy Garrett
Sherman Bagley (Viv's son): Ralph Hart
Mr. Barnsdahl (Danfield Bank president, 1962–63):
    Charles Lane
Harry Connors (Lucy's neighbor, an airplane pilot):
    Dick Martin
Theodore J. Mooney (Danfield Bank president):
    Gale Gordon
Harrison Cheever (Westland Bank president): Roy Roberts
Mary Jane Lewis (Lucy's friend in California):
    Mary Jane Croft

Staff

Executive Producers: Desi Arnaz (1962), Elliott Lewis
Producers: Elliott Lewis, Jack Donohue, Tommy Thompson
Directors: Jack Donohue, Maury Thompson
Writers: Bob Carroll, Jr., Madelyn Pugh Davis, Bob Schiller,
    Bob Weiskopf, Milt Josefsberg, Ray Singer, Bob O'Brien,
    Alan Levitt, Phil Leslie, Gary Marshall, Jerry Belson,
    and others
Music: Wilbur Hatch
Photography: Nick Musuraca, Maury Gertsman
Makeup: Hal King, Lee Greenway

♥   ♥   ♥

"The Lucy Show" Story

Lucy Carmichael, a widowed mother of two children, Chris and Jerry, shares her Danfield, Connecticut, home with her best friend, Vivian Bagley, a divorcée, and Viv's son, Sherman. Together, Lucy and Viv dream up one harebrained scheme after another to save or make money. Whether they go into business selling caramel corn, buy a sheep to keep the grass trimmed, or open their own restaurant, something inevitably goes awry. For instance, when the ladies decide to climb a ladder and install a TV antenna on their own, the result is a hole in the roof and a redhead stuck in the chimney.

Despite the demands of raising their children alone and working as Danfield volunteer firefighters, Lucy and Viv manage to find time to do things for themselves. They build a rumpus room, take judo lessons, play softball, and enroll in an introduction to chemistry and physics class at the local university. While at the university, Lucy attempts to discover the secret of eternal youth after Professor Vance tells her that "anything is possible in the world of science."

As two single women, they also make time for the dating scene. And eventually Vivian lands Mr. Right. With a new husband and stepfather for her son, Vivian says good-bye to her closest friend. The two have had a lot of fun together over the years, and although Viv promises to come back to visit, Lucy knows her life will never be the same.

Shortly after Viv leaves, Jerry expresses an interest in a California military school. Since Chris is already away at college, Lucy decides to move to California to be closer to her son. Besides, her relationship with Mr. Mooney, the Danfield Bank president, has been less than ideal. Here's a chance to get a fresh start in a new place and find a new banker.

After getting settled in her California apartment, Lucy pays a visit to the Westland Bank, whose president, Harrison Cheever, welcomes her and informs her that her account will be overseen by their new vice-president, Mr. Theodore J. Mooney! In a typical "Lucy" twist of fate, Mr. Mooney has accepted a promotion that requires him to relocate to the very bank where Lucy has transferred her account. It doesn't take long before Lucy finagles a job at the bank and becomes Mr. Mooney's secretary.

♥   ♥   ♥

"The Lucy Show" Trivia

♥ Lucy Carmichael's Connecticut address: 132 Post Road, Danfield

♥ Lucie Arnaz appears for the first time on "The Lucy Show" in episode 23, "Lucy is a Soda Jerk." Lucie plays Cynthia, a friend of Lucy's TV daughter, Chris. She appears again in episode 27, "Lucy Is a Chaperone."

♥ Marge is Lucy's only sister.

♥ "The Lucy Show" was based on the book *Life Without George* by Irene Kampen.

♥ Vivian's ex-husband's name is Ralph.

♥ In California, Lucy lives at 780 N. Gower Street in the Glen Hall Apartments.

♥   ♥   ♥

"The Lucy Show" Episode Titles and Original Air Dates

1. "Lucy Waits up for Chris" (10/1/62)
2. "Lucy Buys a Sheep" (10/29/62)
3. "Lucy Digs up a Date" (10/8/62)
4. "Lucy Is a Referee" (10/15/62)
5. "Lucy Misplaces Two Thousand Dollars" (10/22/62)
6. "Lucy Becomes an Astronaut" (11/5/62)
7. "Lucy Is a Kangaroo for a Day" (11/12/62)
8. "Lucy, the Music Lover" (11/19/62)
9. "Lucy Puts up a TV Antenna" (11/26/62)
10. "Lucy Builds a Rumpus Room" (12/10/62)
11. "Vivian Sues Lucy" (12/3/62)
12. "Together for Christmas" (12/24/62)
13. "Chris's New Year's Eve Party" (12/31/62)
14. "Lucy's Sister Pays a Visit" (1/7/63)
15. "Lucy and Her Electric Mattress" (12/17/62)
16. "Lucy and Viv Are Volunteer Firemen" (1/14/63)
17. "Lucy Becomes a Reporter" (1/21/63)
18. "Lucy and Viv Put In a Shower" (1/28/63)
19. "Lucy and Viv Become Tycoons" (2/11/63)
20. "Lucy's Barbershop Quartet" (2/4/63)
21. "No More Double Dates" (2/18/63)
22. "Lucy and Viv Learn Judo" (2/25/63)
23. "Lucy Is a Soda Jerk" (3/4/63)
24. "Lucy Drives a Dump Truck" (3/11/63)
25. "Lucy Visits the White House" (3/25/63)
26. "Lucy and Viv Take Up Chemistry" (4/1/63)
27. "Lucy Is a Chaperone" (4/8/63)
28. "Lucy and the Little League" (4/15/63)
29. "Lucy and the Runaway Butterfly" (4/22/63)
30. "Lucy Buys a Boat" (4/29/63)
31. "Lucy Goes Duck Hunting" (11/4/63)
32. "Lucy and Viv Play Softball" (10/14/63)
33. "Lucy Gets Locked in the Vault" (10/21/63)
34. "Lucy and the Bank Scandal" (11/11/63)
35. "Lucy Plays Cleopatra" (9/30/63)
36. "Kiddie Parties, Inc." (10/7/63)
37. "Lucy and the Safecracker" (10/28/63)
38. "Lucy Decides to Redecorate" (11/18/63)
39. "Lucy Conducts the Symphony" (12/30/63)
40. "The Loophole in the Lease" (12/23/63)
41. "Lucy Puts Out a Fire at the Bank" (12/2/63)
42. "Lucy and the Military Academy" (12/9/63)
43. "Lucy's College Reunion" (12/16/63)
44. "Lucy Teaches Ethel Merman to Sing" (2/3/64)
45. "Lucy Plays Florence Nightingale" (1/6/64)
46. "Lucy Goes to Art Class" (1/13/64)
47. "Chris Goes Steady" (1/20/64)
48. "Ethel Merman and the Boy Scout Show" (2/10/64)
49. "Lucy Takes Up Golf" (1/27/64)
50. "Lucy and Viv Open a Restaurant" (2/17/64)
51. "Lucy Takes a Job at the Bank" (2/24/64)
52. "Viv Moves Out" (3/2/64)
53. "Lucy Is Her Own Lawyer" (3/9/64)
54. "Lucy Meets a Millionaire" (3/16/64)
55. "Lucy Goes into Politics" (3/23/64)
56. "Lucy and the Scout Trip" (3/30/64)
57. "Lucy Is a Process Server" (4/20/64)
58. "Lucy Enters a Baking Contest" (4/27/64)
59. "Lucy, the Good Skate" (9/21/64)
60. "Lucy, the Meter Maid" (11/2/64)
61. "Lucy Tries Winter Sports" (10/5/64)
62. "Lucy and the Great Bank Robbery" (10/19/64)
63. "Lucy Meets Danny Kaye" (12/28/64)
64. "Lucy, the Camp Cook" (10/26/64)
65. "Lucy Gets Amnesia" (10/12/64)
66. "Lucy and the Plumber" (9/28/64)
67. "Lucy Becomes a Father" (11/16/64)
68. "Lucy Makes a Pinch" (11/9/64)
69. "Lucy's Contact Lenses" (11/23/64)
70. "Lucy and the Missing Stamp" (12/21/64)
71. "Lucy, the Coin Collector" (12/14/64)
72. "Lucy, the Disk Jockey" (4/12/65)
73. "Lucy Gets the Bird" (12/7/64)
74. "Lucy Gets Her Maid" (11/30/64)
75. "Lucy and the Monsters" (1/25/65)
76. "Lucy and the Ceramic Cat" (1/11/65)
77. "Lucy Goes to Vegas" (1/18/65)
78. "Lucy and the Countess" (2/1/65)
79. "My Fair Lucy" (2/8/65)
80. "Lucy and the Countess Lose Weight" (2/15/65)

From the animated opening credits of "The Lucy Show," 1962–63

81. "Lucy and Arthur Godfrey" (3/8/65)
82. "Lucy, the Stockholder" (3/29/65)
83. "Lucy and the Beauty Doctor" (3/22/65)
84. "Lucy and the Old Mansion" (3/1/65)
85. "Lucy and the Golden Greek" (9/20/65)
86. "Lucy at Marineland" (9/13/65)
87. "Lucy and Joan" (10/11/65)
88. "Lucy, the Stunt Man" (10/18/65)
89. "Lucy in the Music World" (9/27/65)
90. "Lucy Helps the Countess" (11/8/65)
91. "Lucy and the Sleeping Beauty" (11/15/65)
92. "Lucy Helps Danny Thomas" (11/1/65)
93. "Lucy and the Countess Have a Horse Guest" (10/25/65)
94. "Lucy and the Undercover Agent" (11/22/65)
95. "Lucy and the Return of Iron Man" (11/29/65)
96. "Lucy Saves Milton Berle" (12/6/65)
97. "Lucy Bags a Bargain" (1/17/66)
98. "Lucy, the Choirmaster" (12/13/65)
99. "Lucy Discovers Wayne Newton" (12/27/65)
100. "Lucy and Art Linkletter" (1/10/66)
101. "Lucy, the Rain Goddess" (1/3/66)
102. "Lucy Meets Mickey Rooney" (1/24/66)
103. "Lucy and the Soap Opera" (1/31/66)
104. "Lucy Goes to a Hollywood Premiere" (2/7/66)
105. "Lucy Dates Dean Martin" (2/14/66)
106. "Lucy and Bob Crane" (2/21/66)
107. "Lucy, the Robot" (2/28/66)
108. "Lucy and Clint Walker" (3/7/66)
109. "Lucy, the Gun Moll" (3/14/66)
110. "Lucy, the Superwoman" (3/21/66)
111. "Lucy and George Burns" (9/12/66)
112. "Lucy, the Bean Queen" (9/26/66)
113. "Lucy and the Ring-a-Ding Ring" (10/10/66)
114. "Lucy Gets a Roommate" (10/31/66)
115. "Lucy and Carol in Palm Springs" (11/7/66)
116. "Lucy and the Submarine" (9/19/66)
117. "Lucy Gets Caught in the Draft" (11/14/66)
118. "Lucy and Paul Winchell" (10/3/66)

119. "Lucy and John Wayne" (11/21/66)
120. "Lucy Goes to London" (10/17/66)
121. "Lucy and Pat Collins" (11/28/66)
122. "Mooney the Monkey" (12/5/66)
123. "Lucy and Phil Silvers" (12/12/66)
124. "Lucy's Substitute Secretary" (1/2/67)
125. "Viv Visits Lucy" (1/9/67)
126. "Lucy, the Babysitter" (1/16/67)
127. "Main Street, U.S.A." (1/23/67)
128. "Lucy Puts Main Street on the Map" (1/30/67)
129. "Lucy Meets the Law" (2/13/67)
130. "Lucy, the Fight Manager" (2/20/67)
131. "Lucy Meets Sheldon Leonard" (3/6/67)
132. "Lucy and Tennessee Ernie Ford" (2/27/67)
133. "Lucy Gets Trapped" (9/18/67)
134. "Lucy and the French Movie Star" (9/25/67)
135. "Little Old Lucy" (10/23/67)
136. "Lucy, the Star Maker" (10/2/67)
137. "Lucy Meets the Berles" (9/11/67)
138. "Lucy Gets Jack Benny's Account" (10/16/67)
139. "Lucy and Robert Goulet" (10/30/67)
140. "Lucy Gets Her Diploma" (10/9/67)
141. "Lucy Gets Mooney Fired" (11/6/67)
142. "Lucy Sues Mooney" (11/27/67)
143. "Lucy Gets Involved" (1/15/68)
144. "Lucy, the Philanthropist" (11/20/67)
145. "Lucy and Carol Burnett, Part 1" (12/4/67)
146. "Lucy and Carol Burnett, Part 2" (12/11/67)
147. "Lucy's Mystery Guest" (11/13/67)
148. "Lucy and the Pool Hustler" (1/8/68)
149. "Lucy and Viv Reminisce" (1/1/68)
150. "Lucy and Phil Harris" (2/5/68)
151. "Mooney's Other Wife" (1/22/68)
152. "Lucy and the Stolen Stole" (1/29/68)
153. "Lucy Helps Ken Berry" (2/19/68)
154. "Lucy and the Lost Star" (2/26/68)
155. "Lucy and Sid Caesar" (3/4/68)
156. "Lucy and 'The Boss of the Year' Award" (3/11/68)

"Here's Lucy"

CBS
Situation Comedy
30 Minutes
144 Episodes
Debuted: September 23, 1968
Left prime time: September 2, 1974

Cast

Lucy Carter: Lucille Ball
Harrison Otis Carter (Lucy's brother-in-law): Gale Gordon
Kim Carter (Lucy's daughter): Lucie Arnaz
Craig Carter (Lucy's son): Desi Arnaz, Jr.
Mary Jane Lewis (Lucy's friend): Mary Jane Croft
Vivian Jones (Lucy's friend; guest appearances):
   Vivian Vance

Staff

Executive Producer: Gary Morton
Producers: Cleo Smith, Tommy Thompson
Directors: Jack Baker, Lucille Ball, Jack Carter, Danny

Dayton, Jack Donohue, Herbert Kenwith, George Marshall, Ross Martin, Jerry Paris, Coby Ruskin, Charles Walters, and others

Writers: George Balzer, Vincent Bogert, Bob Carroll, Jr., Madelyn Davis, Lou Derman, Mel Diamond, Ben Gershman, Fred S. Fox, Frank Gill, Jr., Ralph Goodman, Howard Harris, Seaman Jacobs, Milt Josefsberg, David Ketchum, Phil Leslie, Bob O'Brien, Sam Perrin, Martin A. Ragaway, Larry Rhine, Bruce Shelly, Ray Singer, Al Schwartz, Tommy Thompson, and others

Art Director: Ray Beal
Music: Wilbur Hatch
Photography: Maury Gertsman
Makeup: Hal King, Lee Greenway

♥ ♥ ♥

The "Here's Lucy" Story

Living in Los Angeles with her two children, Kim and Craig, Lucille Carter experiences never a dull moment. As secretary to Harrison Otis Carter, her brother-in-law and owner of Carter's Unique Employment Agency, Lucy's overzealous nature lands her in one crazy situation after another, often leaving the office in shambles. Harry is a crotchety old fellow whose short temper is tested each day at the office as soon a his well-meaning sister-in-law sits down to work.

At home, Lucy tries valiantly to cope with the problems of raising two teenage children, and now that her husband is gone, she often calls upon their Uncle Harry to help out. Her actions on her kids' behalf tend to create more problems than they re-

solve, however. For instance, when she accompanies Craig to take his driver's test, she discovers that her own license has expired and ends up behind the wheel, taking the test herself.

Because she lives in southern California, Lucy manages to wangle meetings with many celebrities. She lunches with Johnny Carson, fixes a faucet with Richard Burton, has tea with Ginger Rogers, and, after breaking her leg skiing, shares a hospital room with Eva Gabor. Lucy makes sure that Vivian, her best friend back east, knows all about the time she spends with her famous "friends." But her boasting backfires when Vivian comes to Los Angeles to take Lucy up on her offer to dine with Lucy's "good friend" Lawrence Welk.

♥ ♥ ♥

"Here's Lucy" Trivia

♥ Lucy's home address: 4863 Valley Lawn Drive, Los Angeles.
♥ Motto of Carter's Unique Employment Agency: "Unusual Jobs for Unusual People."
♥ Lucille Ball's personal secretary, Wanda Clark, appears briefly in episode 40, "Lucy Protects Her Job."

♥ Uncle Harry attended Bullwinkle University.
♥ The first three seasons of "Here's Lucy" were filmed at Paramount; the last three, at Universal.

From the opening credits of "Here's Lucy"

♥　　♥　　♥

"Here's Lucy" Episode Titles and Original Air Dates

1. "Mod, Mod Lucy" (9/23/68)
2. "Lucy's Birthday" (11/18/68)
3. "Lucy's Working Daughter" (12/2/68)
4. "Lucy, the Conclusion Jumper" (10/21/68)
5. "Lucy and Eva Gabor" (11/11/68)
6. "Lucy Visits Jack Benny" (9/30/68)
7. "Lucy, the Process Server" (10/7/68)
8. "Lucy's Impossible Mission" (10/28/68)
9. "Lucy and Miss Shelley Winters" (10/14/68)
10. "Lucy and the Gold Rush" (12/30/68)
11. "Lucy and the Great Airport Chase" (2/3/69)
12. "Guess Who Owes Lucy $23.50" (12/9/68)
13. "Lucy Sells Craig to Wayne Newton" (11/25/68)
14. "Lucy, the Matchmaker" (12/16/68)
15. "Lucy, the Fixer" (1/6/69)
16. "Lucy Goes on Strike" (1/20/69)
17. "Lucy and the Ex-Con" (1/13/69)
18. "A Date for Lucy" (2/10/69)
19. "Lucy Gets Her Man" (2/24/69)
20. "Lucy, the Shopping Expert" (2/17/69)
21. "Lucy and Carol Burnett" (1/27/69)
22. "Lucy's Safari" (3/3/69)
23. "Lucy and Tennessee Ernie's Fun Farm" (3/10/69)
24. "Lucy Helps Craig Get a Driver's License" (3/17/69)
25. "Lucy Goes to the Air Force Academy, Part 1" (9/22/69)
26. "Lucy Goes to the Air Force Academy, Part 2" (9/29/69)
27. "Lucy and the Indian Chief" (10/6/69)
28. "Lucy Runs the Rapids" (10/13/69)
29. "Lucy and Harry's Tonsils" (10/20/69)
30. "Lucy's Burglar Alarm" (11/3/69)
31. "Lucy at the Drive-In Movie" (11/10/69)
32. "Lucy and the Andrews Sisters" (10/27/69)
33. "Lucy and the Used Car Dealer" (11/17/69)
34. "Lucy, the Cement Worker" (11/24/69)
35. "Lucy and Johnny Carson" (12/1/69)
36. "Lucy and the Generation Gap" (12/8/69)
37. "Lucy and the Bogie Affair" (12/15/69)
38. "Lucy, the Laundress" (1/12/70)
39. "Lucy, the Helpful Mother" (12/29/69)
40. "Lucy Protects Her Job" (12/22/69)
41. "Lucy and Wayne Newton" (2/16/70)
42. "Lucy and Liberace" (1/5/70)
43. "Lucy and Lawrence Welk" (1/19/70)
44. "Lucy and Viv Visit Tijuana" (1/26/70)
45. "Lucy and Ann-Margret" (2/2/70)
46. "Lucy and Wally Cox" (2/9/70)
47. "Lucy Takes Over" (2/23/70)
48. "Lucy and Carol Burnett" (3/2/70)
49. "Lucy Cuts Vincent's Price" (11/9/70)
50. "Lucy Loses Her Cool" (12/7/70)
51. "Lucy, the Crusader" (10/12/70)
52. "Lucy, the Skydiver" (9/21/70)
53. "Lucy and Sammy Davis, Jr." (9/28/70)
54. "Lucy, the Diamond Cutter" (11/16/70)
55. "Lucy and Jack Benny's Biography" (11/23/70)
56. "Lucy and Ma Parker" (12/21/70)
57. "Lucy and the Drum Contest" (10/5/70)
58. "Lucy Meets the Burtons" (9/14/70)
59. "Lucy Stops a Marriage" (12/28/70)
60. "Lucy Goes Hawaiian, Part 1" (2/15/71)
61. "Lucy Goes Hawaiian, Part 2" (2/22/71)
62. "Lucy, the American Mother" (10/26/70)
63. "Lucy's Wedding Party" (11/2/70)
64. "Lucy and the 20-20 Vision" (1/11/71)
65. "Lucy, the Co-Ed" (10/19/70)
66. "Lucy and Aladdin's Lamp" (2/1/71)

67. "Lucy, Part-Time Wife" (12/14/70)
68. "Lucy and Rudy Vallee" (11/30/70)
69. "Lucy's Vacation" (1/4/71)
70. "Lucy's House Guest, Harry" (1/25/71)
71. "Lucy and Carol Burnett" (2/8/71)
72. "Lucy and the Raffle" (1/18/71)
73. "Lucy and Mannix Are Held Hostage" (10/4/71)
74. "Lucy and Candid Camera" (12/13/71)
75. "Lucy and Harry's Italian Bombshell" (9/27/71)
76. "Lucy Makes a Few Extra Dollars" (10/18/71)
77. "Lucy and the Astronauts" (10/11/71)
78. "Lucy and Her All-Nun Band" (11/1/71)
79. "Someone's on the Ski Lift with Dinah" (10/25/71)
80. "Lucy, the Mountain Climber" (9/20/71)
81. "Lucy and Flip Go Legit" (9/13/71)
82. "Lucy and the Celebrities" (11/15/71)
83. "Lucy's Lucky Day" (12/20/71)
84. "Ginger Rogers Comes to Tea" (11/8/71)
85. "Won't You Calm Down, Dan Dailey?" (11/22/71)
86. "Lucy's Bonus Bounces" (12/27/71)
87. "Lucy Helps David Frost Go Night Night" (11/29/71)
88. "Lucy in the Jungle" (12/6/71)
89. "Lucy and the Chinese Curse" (1/10/72)
90. "Kim Moves Out" (1/24/72)
91. "Lucy Sublets the Office" (1/31/72)
92. "Lucy and the Little Old Lady" (1/3/72)
93. "Lucy's Replacement" (1/17/72)
94. "With Viv as a Friend, Who Needs an Enemy?" (2/21/72)
95. "Lucy's Punctured Romance" (2/7/72)
96. "Kim Finally Cuts You-Know-Who's Apron Strings" (2/28/72)
97. "Lucy and Eva Gabor Are Hospital Roomies" (9/18/72)
98. "Lucy's Big Break" (9/11/72)
99. "Harrison Carter, Male Nurse" (9/25/72)
100. "A Home Is Not an Office" (10/2/72)
101. "Lucy and Joe Namath" (10/9/72)
102. "Lucy and Petula Clark" (10/30/72)
103. "Lucy, the Other Woman" (10/23/72)
104. "The Case of the Reckless Wheelchair Driver" (10/16/72)
105. "Lucy and the Group Encounter" (12/18/72)

106. "Lucy and Donny Osmond" (11/20/72)
107. "Goodbye, Mrs. Hips" (2/26/73)
108. "Dirty Gertie" (11/13/72)
109. "The Not-So-Popular Mechanics" (2/19/73)
110. "Lucy and Jim Bailey" (11/6/72)
111. "Lucy and Her Prince Charming" (11/27/72)
112. "Lucy Is Really in a Pickle" (1/1/73)
113. "Lucy and Her Genuine Twimby" (1/15/73)
114. "My Fair Buzzi" (12/11/72)
115. "Lucy Goes to Prison" (1/22/73)
116. "Lucy Goes on Her Last Blind Date" (1/8/73)
117. "Lucy and the Franchise Fiasco" (2/5/73)
118. "Lucy and the Professor" (1/29/73)
119. "Lucy and Uncle Harry's Pot" (2/12/73)
120. "Lucy and Harry's Memoirs" (3/5/73)
121. "Lucy Plays Cops and Robbers" (11/26/73)
122. "Lucy, the Peacemaker" (9/24/73)
123. "The Big Game" (9/17/73)
124. "Lucy, the Wealthy Widow" (10/1/73)
125. "The Bow-Wow Boutique" (10/8/73)
126. "Lucy and Danny Thomas" (9/10/73)
127. "Lucy's Tenant" (10/22/73)
128. "Lucy Gives Eddie Albert the Old Song and Dance" (10/15/73)
129. "Lucy and Andy Griffith" (10/29/73)
130. "Lucy and Joan Rivers Do Jury Duty" (11/5/73)
131. "Tipsy Through the Tulips" (11/12/73)
132. "The Carters Meet Frankie Avalon" (11/19/73)
133. "Harry Catches Gold Fever" (12/3/73)
134. "Lucy Is a Bird-Sitter" (1/7/74)
135. "Lucy and Chuck Connors Have a Surprise Slumber Party" (12/17/73)
136. "Meanwhile, Back at the Office" (1/14/74)
137. "Lucy Is N. G. as an R. N." (1/21/74)
138. "Lucy, the Sheriff" (1/28/74)
139. "Milton Berle Is the Life of the Party" (2/11/74)
140. "Mary Jane's Boyfriend" (2/18/74)
141. "Lucy Carter Meets Lucille Ball" (3/4/74)
142. "Lucy and Phil Harris Strike Up the Band" (2/25/74)
143. "Where Is My Wandering Mother Tonight?" (3/11/74)
144. "Lucy Fights the System" (3/18/74)

"Life with Lucy"

ABC
Situation Comedy
30 Minutes
13 Episodes
Debuted: September 20, 1986
Left prime time: November 15, 1986

Cast

Lucy Barker: Lucille Ball
Curtis McGibbon (Lucy's brother-in-law): Gale Gordon
Margo McGibbon (Lucy's daughter): Ann Dusenberry
Ted McGibbon (Lucy's son-in-law): Larry Anderson
Becky McGibbon (Lucy's granddaughter): Jenny Lewis
Kevin McGibbon (Lucy's grandson): Philip J. Amelio, II
Leonard Stoner (M & B Hardware store employee):
Donovan Scott

Staff

Executive Producers: Aaron Spelling, Gary Morton,
Douglas S. Cramer
Supervising Producer: E. Duke Vincent
Producers: Madelyn Davis; Bob Carroll, Jr.
Co-Producers: Linda Morris, Vic Rauseo
Directors: Peter Baldwin, Marc Daniels, Bruce Bilson
Writers: Bob Carroll, Jr., Madelyn Davis, Linda Morris,
Vic Rauseo, Arthur Marx, Robert Fisher, Mark Tuttle,
Richard Albrecht, Casey Keller, and others
Music and Lyrics: Martin Silvestri, Jeremy Stone,
Joel Higgins
Theme Song Vocals: Eydie Gorme
Director of Photography: Charles F. Wheeler
Makeup: Fred Williams, Claude Thompson

♥   ♥   ♥

The "Life with Lucy" Story

After her husband's death, Lucy Barker takes his place as co-owner of the M & B Hardware store in Pasadena. To the dismay of her husband's longtime business partner, Curtis McGibbon, Lucy begins to give the store a brand-new look. In order to find everything more easily, she decides to rearrange the stock alphabetically—air fresheners before alarm clocks and blenders after batteries. An industrial-size fire extinguisher is soon installed, and a guard goose is added to the payroll to patrol the store at night. When Lucy has an unfriendly computer hooked up to make M & B more efficient, Curtis has no choice but to learn all about floppy disks.

As if contending with Lucy at the store weren't exasperating enough, Curtis must put up with her on the home front as well because her daughter, Margo, is married to his son, Ted. And when Curtis learns that Lucy has decided to move in with Ted and Margo so she can spend more time with her grandchildren, Becky and Kevin, he moves in too. He fears that his grandchildren might pick up some of Grandma Barker's goofy traits if he isn't around to watch over them.

At home, Lucy introduces the family to organic energizer drinks, talks to her plants, teaches Becky how to play the saxophone, brings home comedian John Ritter after an unfortunate accident at the store, and gets into a frosting fight with her visiting sister when the two don't see eye-to-eye. Every day is an adventure when you're living your life with Lucy.

From the opening credits of "Life with Lucy," 1986

♥ ♥ ♥

"Life with Lucy" Trivia

♥ M & B Hardware address: 7207 Hill Street, Pasadena, CA 91106
♥ Lucy's husband's name was Sam Barker.
♥ Lucy and Curtis once appeared on "Wake-Up Pasadena," a local morning TV show.
♥ Audrey is Lucy's only sister; Margo is Lucy's only daughter.
♥ Kevin is on the Wildcats soccer team.

♥ M & B Hardware has been in business for 36 years.
♥ Lucy's maiden name is Everett.
♥ Lucy Barker once appeared on stage in *A Soldier's Song* at the Pasadena Playhouse.
♥ Curtis's wife's name was Josephine.
♥ Ted and Margo have been married for ten years.

♥ ♥ ♥

"Life with Lucy" Episode Titles and Original Air Dates

1. "One Good Grandparent Deserves Another" (9/20/86)
2. "Lucy and the Guard Goose"*
3. "Lucy Gets Her Wires Crossed" (10/18/86)
4. "Lucy Makes a Hit with John Ritter" (9/27/86)
5. "Lucy Is a Sax Symbol" (10/25/86)
6. "Love among the Two-By-Fours" (10/4/86)
7. "Lucy and Curtis Are up a Tree"*
8. "Lucy Makes Curtis Byte the Dust" (11/1/86)
9. "Lucy's Green Thumb"*

10. "Lucy, Legal Eagle" (11/8/86)
11. "Breaking Up Is Hard to Do"*
12. "Mother of the Bride" (11/15/86)
13. "World's Greatest Grandma"
14. "'Twas the Flight before Christmas"**

*unaired episode
**unfilmed episode

Lucille Ball Filmography

(in alphabetical order by year of release)
*unbilled role

1. *Blood Money** (Fox/United Artists, 1933). Elaine Talbot (Frances Dee), a rich young woman, falls in love with Bill Bailey (George Bancroft), a gangster. (Crime drama, 66 minutes, b/w)

2. *The Bowery** (20th Century, 1933). Chuck Connors (Wallace Beery) is the owner of a saloon in this drama of jealousy and competition between rival gangs. (Drama, 92 minutes, b/w)

3. *Broadway Thru a Keyhole** (20th Century/United Artists, 1933). Frank Rocci (Paul Kelly) is shot while rescuing Joan Whelan (Constance Cummings), a nightclub girl, from kidnappers. While lying in the hospital, Rocci hears Walter Winchell praise him for his courageous act and learns that his rival for Joan's heart is dead. Note: Look closely for a blond Lucille in the beach scene. (Drama, 90 minutes, b/w)

4. *Roman Scandals** (Goldwyn/United Artists, 1933). Eddie (Eddie Cantor), a delivery boy from Oklahoma, daydreams about life in ancient Rome. Note: Lucille, dressed only in a long blond wig, appears as one of the slave girls. (Musical comedy, 87 minutes, b/w)

5. *The Affairs of Cellini** (20th Century/United Artists, 1934). Constance Bennett stars as the Duchess of Florence in this film about Renaissance artist Benvenuto Cellini (Fredric March), who is attracted to other men's wives. (Comedy, 90 minutes, b/w)

6. *Bottoms Up** (Fox, 1934). Spencer Tracy stars as Smoothie King, a slick talent agent who claims his client is an English lord ready to win the hearts of American audiences. (Musical, 85 minutes, b/w)

7. *Broadway Bill** (Columbia, 1934). Warner Baxter (Dan Brooks) abandons his wife and her family's business for a new life as owner of a racehorse. Also known as *Strictly Confidential*. (Comedy, 104 minutes, b/w)

8. *Bulldog Drummond Strikes Back** (Goldwyn/United Artists, 1934). Lola Field (Loretta Young) searches for her missing aunt and uncle in this mystery, one in a series of *Bulldog Drummond* films. (Mystery, 83 minutes, b/w)

9. *The Fugitive Lady** (Columbia, 1934). Florence Rice stars as Ann Duncan, a wife-to-be who learns that her fiancé is a jewel thief and she, his accomplice. Note: Lucille Ball plays one of the beauty operators. (Drama, 66 minutes, b/w)

10. *Hold That Girl** (Fox, 1934). A reporter, Tony Bellamy (Claire Trevor) gets mixed up in a police raid and is mistakenly hauled into court. (Comedy, 70 minutes, b/w)

11. *Jealousy** (Columbia, 1934). After killing his wife's boss in a jealous rage, boxer Larry O'Roark (George Murphy) is sentenced to die in the electric chair. Just before he meets his fate, O'Roark awakens to find himself lying on his back in a boxing ring. Note: Lucille Ball was cast as "the girl." (Drama, 66 minutes, b/w)

12. *Kid Millions** (Goldwyn/United Artists, 1934). Another Eddie Cantor film. This time Eddie goes to a foreign land to claim the inheritance his archaeologist father left him. Note: Lucille appears as one of the Goldwyn Girls in "Ice Cream Fantasy," the final musical number, which was filmed in Technicolor. Ethel Merman and Ann Sothern also appear in the film. (Musical, 90 minutes, b/w and color)

13. *Men of the Night** (Columbia, 1934). Car-chasing crime drama starring Bruce Cabot as Kelly, an undercover detective assigned to catch a group of Hollywood jewel thieves. Note: Lucy plays the role of Peggy. (Drama, 58 minutes, b/w)

14. *Moulin Rouge** (20th Century/United Artists, 1934). In an effort to revitalize her marriage and career, Helen Hall (Constance Bennett) attempts to impersonate her sister. Note: Look for Lucille in the nightclub scenes. (Musical, 64 minutes, b/w)

15. *Murder at the Vanities** (Paramount, 1934). Bill Murdock (Victor MacLaglean) is the investigator trying to solve a mysterious series of back-stage murders during an opening night. (Musical/Mystery, 89 minutes, b/w)

16. *Nana** (Goldwyn/United Artists, 1934). Anna Sten plays Nana, a French entertainer who takes her own life in order to bring two brothers together. Also known as *The Lady of the Boulevards*. Note: Lucille Ball appears as a chorus girl. (Drama, 89 minutes, b/w)

17. *Carnival* (Columbia, 1935). Lee Tracy stars as Chick Thompson, a carnival puppeteer whose wife has died while giving birth to their son. When the authorities decide that the carnival is not an appropriate environment to raise little Poochy (Dickie Walters), Thompson kidnaps his son from the hospital and begins avoiding the police. Note: Lucille Ball appears as a nurse in the hospital scene. This

was her first credited movie and her last film before being dropped by Columbia. Jimmy Durante costars. (Comedy/Drama, 77 minutes, b/w)

18. *I Dream Too Much* (RKO, 1935). When Annette Street (Lily Pons) finds success as an opera singer, her husband, Jonathan (Henry Fonda), a struggling composer, becomes jealous. Note: Lucille has a small role as wisecracking Gwendolyn Dilley. (Musical, 97 minutes, b/w)

19. *Old Man Rhythm** (RKO, 1935) When Johnny Roberts (Buddy Rogers) goes to college, his father (George Barbier) enrolls as well to keep a watchful eye on his son's romances. Note: Look for Lucy as one of the college girls here. (Musical, 74 minutes, b/w)

20. *Roberta** (RKO, 1935). A story of romance about Huckleberry Haines (Fred Astaire) and Lizzie Gatz (Ginger Rogers), who rekindle an affair after meeting unexpectedly in Paris. Note: Lucille appears as a model in the film's final scene. (Musical, 105 minutes, b/w)

21. *Top Hat** (RKO, 1935) In this Astaire-Rogers musical, a woman (Ginger Rogers) mistakenly believes that the dancer (Fred Astaire) who is wooing her is already married. Note: Watch for Lucille Ball as the flower shop clerk. (Musical, 99 minutes, b/w)

22. *The Three Musketeers** (RKO, 1935). Three loyal swashbucklers battle Cardinal Richelieu in this film based on the classic Alexandre Dumas novel. (Adventure, 97 minutes, b/w)

23. *The Whole Town's Talking** (Columbia, 1935). Arthur Jones (Edward G. Robinson), a shy store clerk, has the incredibly bad luck of looking just like a certain escaped criminal. (Comedy, 95 minutes, b/w)

24. *Bunker Bean* (RKO, 1936). After meeting with a fortune teller, stenographer Bunker Bean (Owen Davis, Jr.) learns to overcome his inferiorities. Note: Lucille plays Miss Kelly. Hedda Hopper also appears. (Comedy, 65 minutes, b/w)

25. *Chatterbox* (RKO, 1936). Anne Shirley stars as Jenny Yates, a star-struck Vermont farm girl whose grandfather tries to discourage her from becoming an actress. Note: Lucille plays Lillian Temple. (Drama, 68 minutes, b/w)

26. *The Farmer in the Dell* (RKO, 1936). Pa Boyer (Fred Stone), an Iowa farmer, moves his family to Hollywood in hopes that his daughter will be "discovered." Note: Lucille plays Gloria, the script girl. (Comedy, 67 minutes, b/w)

27. *Follow the Fleet* (RKO, 1936). Bake Baker (Fred Astaire) decides to join the Navy after his love, Sherry Martin (Ginger Rogers), rejects his marriage proposal. Note: Lucille plays Kitty Collins. (Musical, 110 minutes, b/w)

28. *Don't Tell the Wife* (RKO, 1937). Simple-minded newspaper editor Malcolm Winthrop (Guy Kibbee) invests in a gold mine that proves to be legitimate. Note: Lucille plays Ann Howell. Also, look for Hattie McDaniel playing a maid two years prior to portraying Mammy in *Gone with the Wind*. (Comedy, 64 minutes, b/w)

29. *Stage Door* (RKO, 1937). Lucille Ball, Katharine Hepburn, Ginger Rogers, Eve Arden, and Ann Miller play aspiring actresses all residing at the Footlights Club in New York,

hoping to make it big on Broadway. Note: Lucille plays Judy Canfield, an actress who gives up her career to be with the man she loves. (Comedy/Drama, 87 minutes, b/w)

30. *That Girl from Paris* (RKO, 1937). Nikki Martin (Lily Pons), a French opera singer, stows away on a ship, joins an American band, hides from immigration officials, and falls in love. Note: Lucille plays Claire Williams. (Musical, 110 minutes, b/w)

31. *Winterset** (RKO, 1937). Burgess Meredith stars as Mio, the son of an Italian immigrant executed for a crime he didn't commit. Convinced of his father's innocence, Mio sets out to uncover the truth. Note: Lucille Ball and Barbara Pepper are cast as extras. (Drama, 78 minutes, b/w)

32. *The Affairs of Annabel* (RKO, 1938). Annabel Allison (Lucille) is a fast-fading movie star who will do just about anything to be noticed. After being talked into some wild publicity stunts by her agent, Lanny Morgan (Jack Oakie), Annabel lands in jail. Originally titled *The Menial Star*. (Comedy, 68 minutes, b/w)

33. *Annabel Takes a Tour* (RKO, 1938). This sequel sends Annabel Allison (Lucille) on a personal appearance tour for her latest film, during which she falls in love with a novelist. (Comedy, 67 minutes, b/w)

34. *Go Chase Yourself* (RKO, 1938). Bank teller Wilbur Meely (Joe Penner) is held hostage in a trailer being pulled by robbers. Wilbur's wife, Carol (Lucille), and the police both believe Wilbur robbed the bank. Note: *Go Chase Yourself* was Lucille's first leading movie role. (Comedy, 70 minutes, b/w)

35. *Having Wonderful Time* (RKO, 1938). Teddy Shaw (Ginger Rogers), bored with her life in the big city, takes a summer vacation in the Catskills, where she romances Chick Kirkland (Douglas Fairbanks, Jr.). Note: Lucille plays Miriam, one of Rogers's roommates. Also look for Red Skelton playing Itchy Faulkner in his motion picture debut. (Musical, 70 minutes, b/w)

36. *The Joy of Living* (RKO, 1938). After being saved from a mob of fans by Dan Webster (Douglas Fairbanks, Jr.), radio star Maggie Garret (Irene Dunne) decides her family has taken advantage of her long enough. Note: Lucille plays Maggie's sister, Salina. (Comedy, 91 minutes, b/w)

37. *The Next Time I Marry* (RKO, 1938). Nancy Fleming (Lucille) could be one of the country's wealthiest women— all she needs to do is marry a "real American" in order to collect her inheritance. The problem is she's in love with a foreigner. (Comedy, 64 minutes, b/w)

38. *Room Service* (RKO, 1938). Determined to stay in his hotel room until he can come up with enough money to produce his play, producer Gordon Miller (Groucho Marx) promises Christine (Lucille) the starring role. (Comedy, 78 minutes, b/w)

39. *Beauty for the Asking* (RKO, 1939). Jean Russell (Lucille) not only runs a New York cosmetics business but also develops a remarkable skin cream in this flick about facials, mud packs, and hairdos. (Drama, 68 minutes, b/w)

40. *Five Came Back* (RKO, 1939). An airplane crashes in South

America leaving twelve passengers stranded. After repairs are made, it is determined that the plane can carry only five people back safely. As the sound of the native head-hunters' drums continually gets louder, a decision needs to be made about who gets left behind. Note: Lucille plays Peggy, one of the passengers. (Drama, 75 minutes, b/w)

41. *Panama Lady* (RKO, 1939). Lucy (Lucille), a singer in a Panama cabaret, plots to rob McTeague (Allan Lane), a hard-drinking oilman. After getting caught, Lucy becomes McTeague's housekeeper to avoid doing jail time. (Drama, 64 minutes, b/w)

42. *That's Right, You're Wrong* (RKO, 1939). Kay Kyser and his College of Musical Knowledge head to Hollywood to star in their first motion picture, but screenwriters find it difficult to develop an appropriate script for Kyser's character. Everything changes when starlet Sandra Sand (Lucille) falls in love with Kyser's band manager, Chuck Deems (Dennis O'Keefe), and convinces studio execs to include the Kyser clan in her next film. (Musical, 91 minutes, b/w)

43. *Twelve Crowded Hours* (RKO, 1939). Nick Green (Richard Dix), an investigative reporter engaged to Paula Sanders (Lucille), tries to save his fiancée's brother from a life of crime. (Drama, 64 minutes, b/w)

44. *Dance, Girl, Dance* (RKO, 1940). Lucille plays "Bubbles," the more popular dancer in this musical that costars Maureen O'Hara as an out-of-work ballerina who is forced to find work at a burlesque house—where the clientele doesn't appreciate the art of ballet. (Musical, 89 minutes, b/w)

45. *The Marines Fly High* (RKO, 1940). Joan Grant (Lucille), the owner of an American cocoa plantation, is kidnapped by bandits who've raided the plantation. Richard Dix and Chester Morris costar as men fighting for Joan's affection and safe return. (Drama, 68 minutes, b/w)

46. *Too Many Girls* (RKO, 1940). Four football players serve as bodyguards for Connie Casey (Lucille), a spoiled young woman who attends a small college in New Mexico. Note: Desi Arnaz, who starred in *Too Many Girls* on Broadway, was brought out to California to reprise his role as Manuelito for the film, bringing Lucy and Desi together for the first time. (Musical, 85 minutes, b/w)

47. *You Can't Fool Your Wife* (RKO, 1940). Clara Fields (Lucille) and Andrew Hinklin (James Ellison) were members of the 1935 graduating class at Mt. Colony College. The sweethearts marry in hopes of living happily ever after, but five years into their marriage Clara has little to be happy about; she suspects her husband of infidelity and is forced to deal with her mother's constant nagging. (Comedy, 68 minutes, b/w)

48. *A Girl, a Guy, and a Gob* (RKO, 1941). This navy comedy features a crazy love triangle involving Dot Duncan (Lucille), her obnoxious fiancé, "Coffee Cup" (George Murphy), and her shy, rich boss, Stephen Herrick (Edmond O'Brien). Also known as *The Navy Steps Out*. (Comedy, 91 minutes, b/w)

49. *Look Who's Laughing* (RKO, 1941). When an airplane piloted by Edgar Bergen and Charlie McCarthy lands in Wistful Vista, everyone, including Fibber McGee and Molly (Jim and Marian Jordan) is in for a treat. Note: Lucille plays Bergen's assistant, Julie Patterson. Originally titled *Look Who's Talking*. (Comedy, 79 minutes, b/w)

50. *The Big Street* (RKO, 1942). Gloria Lyons (Lucille), a New York nightclub singer, is crippled by her former boyfriend in a fall. Henry Fonda plays "Pinks," a polite young Broadway busboy who becomes infatuated with and cares for the selfish singer as she recuperates. Originally titled *It Comes Up Love*. Note: Agnes Moorhead ("Bewitched") plays Violette in a supporting role. (Drama, 88 minutes, b/w)

51. *Seven Days' Leave* (RKO, 1942). Army private Johnny Grey III (Victor Mature) learns he has seven days to marry into a rich family in order to collect his $100,000 inheritance. He sets his sights on Terry Havalok Allen (Lucille), who's already interested in someone else. (Musical comedy, 87 minutes, b/w)

52. *Valley of the Sun* (RKO, 1942). Christine Larson (Lucille), a restaurant owner, is romanced by two men who have contradicting views on the treatment of the Indians in old Arizona. Note: Lucille's only western found her on location in New Mexico. (Western, 79 minutes, b/w)

53. *Best Foot Forward* (MGM, 1943). Movie star Lucille Ball (as herself) accepts an invitation to a military ball from a fan enlisted at the Winsocki Military Academy and soon finds herself in the middle of a scandal. Note: June Allyson made her film debut in this movie. A young Nancy Walker also has a supporting role. (Musical, 95 minutes, color)

54. *Du Barry Was a Lady* (MGM, 1943). Louis Blore (Red Skelton) is a hatcheck boy who falls in love with nightclub singer May Daly (Lucille). When Louis learns of another man's interest in May, he dreams of becoming King Louis XV—with May as his Madame Du Barry. (Musical comedy, 103 minutes, color)

55. *Thousands Cheer* (MGM, 1943). Eddie Marsh (Gene Kelly) finds Army life unbearable, falls in love with the colonel's daughter (Kathryn Grayson), and attends a USO show featuring Lucille Ball, Red Skelton, Judy Garland, Mickey Rooney, and Ann Sothern. (Musical, 126 minutes, color)

56. *Meet the People* (MGM, 1944). Playwright and welder William "Swanee" Swanson (William Powell) dismisses Julie Hampton (Lucille), a Broadway star, from a play he wrote because he feels she's too conceited for the part. To prove him wrong, Hampton accepts a job at a shipyard to "meet the people" and eventually wins Swanson's heart. (Musical, 99 minutes, b/w)

57. *Abbott and Costello in Hollywood* (MGM, 1945). Bud Abbott and Lou Costello are Hollywood barbers on the loose at Mammoth Movie Studios, where actress Lucille Ball is trying to film a movie. (Comedy, 84 minutes, b/w)

58. *Without Love* (MGM, 1945) Pat Jamieson (Spencer Tracy), a scientist working on a new invention, arrives in Washington, D.C., and ends up marrying Jamie Rowan (Katharine Hepburn) just to share a house. Note: Lucille plays

Kitty Trimble, a wise-cracking real estate agent. (Comedy, 111 minutes, b/w)

59. *The Dark Corner* (20th Century Fox, 1946). Detective Bradford Galt (Mark Stevens) is framed for the murder of his ex-partner. Only his secretary, Kathleen Conley (Lucille), believes he's innocent. (Mystery, 99 minutes, b/w)

60. *Easy to Wed* (MGM, 1946). After an unflattering story of her life-style appears in a newspaper, Connie Allenbury (Esther Williams) threatens to sue newspaperman Warren Haggerty (Keenan Wynn) for libel. Note: Lucille plays the supporting role of Gladys Benton, Haggerty's fiancée. (Musical, 109 minutes, color)

61. *Lover Come Back* (Universal, 1946). After discovering that her war correspondent husband, Bill (George Brent), was fooling around while away, Kay Williams (Lucille) decides to get even and do the same. When her husband doesn't get jealous, Kay is determined to get a quick divorce. Also known as *Lesson in Love* and *When Lovers Meet*. (Comedy, 90 minutes, b/w)

62. *Two Smart People* (MGM, 1946). John Hodiak stars as Ace Connors, a crook about to serve a prison sentence. Lucille costars as Ricki Woodner, who makes the mistake of falling in love with Connors. Originally titled *Time for Two*. (Drama, 93 minutes, b/w)

63. *Ziegfeld Follies of 1946* (MGM, 1946). From his home in heaven, the great Broadway producer/director Florenz Ziegfeld (William Powell) imagines who would have been part of the new Ziegfeld Follies of 1946. Note: Judy Garland, Esther Williams, Keenan Wynn, and William Frawley are among the many guest stars. Lucille appears as a glamorous, whip-cracking lion tamer. (Musical, 110 minutes, color)

64. *Her Husband's Affairs* (Columbia, 1947). William Weldon (Franchot Tone) is an ad man whose loving wife, Margaret (Lucille), always gets the credit for his top-notch work. When William takes on an ad campaign for a wacky inventor, chaos ensues. (Comedy, 84 minutes, b/w)

65. *Lured* (United Artists, 1947). In London, taxi dancer Sandra Carpenter (Lucille) joins forces with Scotland Yard to catch a mysterious killer who attracts women by placing advertisements in the personal columns of newspapers. To nab the killer before he strikes again, Carpenter serves as a decoy. Also known as *Personal Column*. Note: Boris Karloff also stars. (Mystery, 102 minutes, b/w)

66. *Easy Living* (RKO, 1949). Pete Wilson (Victor Mature), a New York Chiefs halfback, is turned down for a coaching position. The team's secretary, Anne (Lucille), offers Wilson support and secretly falls in love with him. (Drama, 77 minutes, b/w)

67. *Miss Grant Takes Richmond* (Columbia, 1949). After attending the Woodruff Secretarial School, Ellen Grant (Lucille) thinks she's been hired as a secretary by a real estate agent. But in reality her employer, Dick Richmond (William Holden), is a con artist who runs an illegal horse-race booking ring in the back office. Also known as *Innocence Is Bliss*. (Comedy/Drama, 87 minutes, b/w)

68. *Sorrowful Jones* (Paramount, 1949). Bob Hope plays Sorrowful Jones, a New York bookie who's given a gambler's young daughter as collateral for an unpaid debt. When the father doesn't return, Sorrowful is forced to care for young Martha Jane (Mary Jane Saunders). Gladys O'Neill (Lucille), a nightclub singer and friend of Sorrowful's, begins spending time with the mismatched pair; eventually they form a family. (Comedy, 88 minutes, b/w)

69. *Fancy Pants* (Paramount, 1950). Believing Humphrey (Bob Hope) is a British lord, Agatha Floud (Lucille) invites him to return to New Mexico with her and serve as the family butler. Humphrey accepts the invitation and plays the charade until Agatha's beau uncovers the truth. (Musical comedy, 92 minutes, color)

70. *The Fuller Brush Girl* (Columbia, 1950). Sally Elliot (Lucille), a door-to-door cosmetics saleslady, innocently gets entangled with crooks, murder, and the law. Also known as *The Affairs of Sally*. Note: Eddie Albert costars as Sally's fiancé, Humphrey Briggs. (Comedy, 87 minutes, b/w)

71. *A Woman of Distinction** (Columbia, 1950). It appears that Susan Middlecott (Rosalind Russell), the dean of a women's college, has no time for romance, at least until a reporter starts spreading some nasty rumors. Note: Lucille appears in an unbilled cameo role. (Comedy, 85 minutes, b/w)

72. *The Magic Carpet* (Columbia, 1951). After learning the secret of the magic carpet, Prince Ramoth (John Agar) persuades a harem girl named Narah (Lucille) to help him free his people from the evil rule of the Caliph. Note: This was Lucille's last film before finding great success in television. (Adventure, 84 minutes, color)

73. *The Long, Long Trailer* (MGM, 1954). Tacy and Nicholas Collini (Lucille Ball and Desi Arnaz) are honeymooners who buy a trailer home and soon encounter the problems of living in a house on wheels. (Comedy, 97 minutes, color)

74. *Forever Darling* (MGM, 1956). Lorenzo Vega (Desi Arnaz), a chemist working on a new insecticide, has been spending too many hours in the lab and too few with his wife, Susan (Lucille). Seeing that their marriage is in trouble, a guardian angel (James Mason) appears to Susan in an attempt to help the couple. (Comedy, 91 minutes, color)

75. *The Facts of Life* (United Artists, 1960). Kitty Weaver and Larry Gilbert (Lucille Ball and Bob Hope) are middle-aged lovers who find adultery to be more trouble than it's worth. (Comedy, 103 minutes, b/w)

76. *Critic's Choice* (Warner Brothers, 1963). Parker Ballantine (Bob Hope), a stubborn New York drama critic, arrives drunk at the Broadway opening of the first play written by his wife, Angela (Lucille). Parker's unflattering review results in an unhappy Ballantine household. (Comedy, 100 minutes, color)

77. *A Guide for the Married Man* (20th Century Fox, 1967). Lucille Ball, Jack Benny, Art Carney, Jayne Mansfield, and others make guest appearances in this Walter Matthau film about a suburban husband who decides to dabble in infidelity. (Comedy, 89 minutes, color)

78. *Yours, Mine and Ours* (United Artists, 1968). After moving to

Abbott and Costello in Hollywood, **MGM, 1945**

northern California with her eight children to start a new life, widow Helen North (Lucille) meets widower Frank Beardsley (Henry Fonda), a Navy warrant officer with ten children of his own. The two fall in love, marry, and learn to cope with the demands of raising eighteen children. Note: *Yours, Mine and Ours* was based on the book *Who Gets the Drumstick?* (Comedy, 111 minutes, color)

79. *Mame* (Warner Brothers, 1974). During Prohibition and the Depression, Mame Dennis (Lucille) tries her hand at show business, marriage, and caring for her orphaned nephew in this film about a dynamic woman who lives life to the fullest. (Musical comedy, 132 minutes, color)

Bibliography

Biographies

Andrews, Bart. *The "I Love Lucy" Book.* New York: Doubleday, 1985.

————. *Lucy & Ricky & Fred & Ethel: The Story of "I Love Lucy."* New York: Dutton, 1976.

Andrews, Bart, and Thomas J. Watson. *Loving Lucy.* New York: St. Martin's Press, 1980.

Arnaz, Desi. *A Book.* New York: William Morrow and Company, 1976.

Brady, Kathleen. *Lucille: The Life of Lucille Ball.* New York: Hyperion, 1994.

Brochu, Jim. *Lucy in the Afternoon.* New York: William Morrow and Company, 1990.

Cohen, Joel H. *Laugh with Lucy.* New York: Scholastic Book Services, 1974.

Gregory, James. *The Lucille Ball Story.* New York: Signet, 1974.

Harris, Eleanor. *The Real Story of Lucille Ball.* New York: Farrar, Straus and Young, 1954.

Harris, Warren G. *Lucy & Desi.* New York: Simon and Schuster, 1991.

Higham, Charles. *Lucy: The Real Life of Lucille Ball.* New York: St. Martin's Press, 1986.

Johnson, Ann D. *Value of Laughter: The Story of Lucille Ball.* San Diego: Value Communications, 1990.

Krohn, Katherine E. *Lucille Ball: Pioneer of Comedy.* Minneapolis: Lerner, 1992.

McClay, Michael. *The Official "I Love Lucy" Book.* New York: Warner, 1995.

McGarry, Annie. *Lucy!* New York: Smithmark, 1993.

Morella, Joe, and Edward Z. Epstein. *Lucy: The Bittersweet Life of Lucille Ball.* Secaucus, N.J.: Lyle Stuart Inc., 1973.

————. *Forever Lucy.* Secaucus, N.J.: Lyle Stuart Inc., 1986.

Paige, David. *Lucille Ball.* Mankato, Minn.: Creative Educational Society, 1977.

Sanders, Coyne Steven, and Tom Gilbert. *Desilu: The Story of Lucille Ball and Desi Arnaz.* New York: William Morrow, 1993.

Turck, Mary. *Lucille Ball.* Mankato, Minn.: Capstone Press, 1989.

Related Books

Andrews, Bart. *The "I Love Lucy" Quiz Book.* San Diego: A. S. Barnes and Company, Inc., 1981.

Beardsley, Helen. *Who Gets the Drumstick?* New York: Bantam, 1968. (The novel on which the film *Yours, Mine and Ours* was based.)

Fannin, Cole. *Lucy and the Madcap Mystery.* Racine, Wis.: Whitman Publishing, 1963.

Fuller, Roger. *The Facts of Life.* New York: Permabooks, 1960.

Kampen, Irene. *Life Without George.* New York: Doubleday, 1961. (The novel on which "The Lucy Show" was based.)

Key, Sarah, Jennifer Newman Brazil, and Vicki Wells. *The "I Love Lucy" Cookbook.* New York: Abbeville Press, 1994.

Rorick, Isabel Scott. *Mr. and Mrs. Cugat.* Boston: Houghton Mifflin Company, 1940. (The novel on which Lucy's radio series, "My Favorite Husband," was based.)

Thibodeaux, Keith, and Audrey Hingley. *Life after Lucy: The True Story of "I Love Lucy's" Little Ricky.* Green Forest, Ark.: New Leaf Press, 1994.

Twiss, Clinton. *The Long, Long Trailer.* New York: Crowell, 1951.

Index

V

V, 140
vacuum cleaners: endorsements for, 81, 92
Valley of the Sun, 211
Vance, Vivian, 154, 188, 195, 199, 204; autographed memorabilia of, 149; comics and, 33, 48–49; on TV-listing magazine covers, 18
vest: ostrich-feather, 162–63
videocassettes, 165, 173
View-Master, 63, 67
Vitameatavegamin doll, 168
Voyager Company catalog, 184

W

Walters, Barbara, 187
Warner Brothers, 71, 77, 78, 129, 212, 213
Warner Brothers Records, 133
watches, 155, 157

Waterloo Daily Courier Family Weekly, 109
Watson, Tom, 165
Wayne, John, 155
Weber Originals, 82
Weistling, Morgan, 167
We Love Lucy: The International Lucille Ball Fan Club, 165, 180–81; letter to members of, 148
"We Love Lucy" buttons, 181
"We Need a Little Christmas," 129
Western Family, 116
Western Printing and Lithographing Co., 33, 36–49, 68–69
Western Union Bunnygrams, 82, 99
Westinghouse, 82, 84, 99
"Westinghouse Lucy-Desi Wonderama Days," 99
Whisper, 105, 120
Whitman Publishing, 51, 60–61, 63, 68–69
Whole Town's Talking, The, 210
Who's Who in TV & Radio, 115
Who-Z-At Star? trading cards, 142
Wildcat, 63, 129, 132, 187
window cards, 71, 78; foreign, 144
Winterset, 210
Wisconsin State Journal TV-Week, 31
Without Love, 75, 211–12

Woman of Distinction, A, 212
Woman's Home Companion, 95
women's magazines, 105, 126–27; foreign, 137
Woodbury beauty products, 90
wristwatches, 155, 157
writing tablets, 147, 152–53

Y

You Can't Fool Your Wife, 211
"You're Nearer" sheet music, 134
Yours, Mine and Ours, 77, 173, 212–13; soundtrack recording of, 129, 132

Z

Zanra Productions, Inc., 48
Zany Toys, Inc., 51, 53
Ziegfeld Follies, 81, 135
Ziegfeld Follies of 1946, 74, 212; soundtrack recording of, 129, 132

Memorabilia Credits

All memorabilia featured in *For the Love Of Lucy* is from the
author's personal collection, with the exception of the following:

Courtesy of Sue Buetow: *The Lucy Show Cut-Out Coloring Book*
(no. 142), page 69.

Courtesy of Pam Gragg: *Beauty for the Asking* lobby card
(no. 174), page 77; *The Dark Corner* lobby card (no. 183),
page 77; *Sorrowful Jones* lobby card (no. 188), page 78;
"Carousel Cookery" cookbook (no. 195), page 84; Star-cal decal (no. 251), page 99; *Uge-Revyen* (nos. 421–23), page 139;
Movie Stars filler paper (no. 483), page 151.

Courtesy of Hake's Americana (York, Penn.): Saalfield paper
dolls (no. 124), page 58; Desi Arnaz toy conga drum (no. 525),
page 161.

Courtesy of Hamilton Gifts (Jacksonville, Fla.): Ricky Ricardo
doll (no. 544), page 168.

Courtesy of Patti Pesavento: "Seein' Stars" newspaper comic
strip (no. 68), page 34; Saalfield paper dolls (no. 125),
page 59; RC Cola swimsuit ad (no. 257), page 102; *Newsweek*
(no. 376), page 126; "Cha-Cha-Cha" sheet music (no. 402),
page 134.

Courtesy of Cari Purkey: "I Love Lucy" baby doll (no. 117),
page 52.

Courtesy of Michael Stern: *The Billboard* (no. 265), page 107;
Pic (no. 291), page 112; *Movie Life* (no. 299), page 113.

Courtesy of Richard Michael Tususian: *Fancy Pants* comic book
(no. 69), page 34; *Miss Beverly Hills of Hollywood* comic
book (no. 70), page 34.

Publicity Still Credits

All publicity stills are from the author's personal collection,
with the exception of the following:

page 2: Courtesy of Lucie Arnaz

page 62: Courtesy of Tom Watson

page 70: Courtesy of Pam Gragg

page 128: Courtesy of Rick Carl

page 193: Courtesy of Gregg Oppenheimer